Dear Friend:

Rarely does a book come along that earns the designation of a must-read "Christian Classic." The volume you are holding in your hands is such a book.

Laurie and I were honored to know Paul Billheimer personally. In the early 1980s I ran camera on his long-running TBN television series based on this very book. I witnessed first-hand the positive influence he had on the foundational theology that helped build TBN — so much so that my parents, TBN founders Paul and Jan Crouch, named a building at our Southern California campus after him.

My dad once said that next to the Bible, *Destined for the Throne* changed and blessed his and my mom's lives more than any other book they ever read. It's safe to say that the principles in this book caused my parents to be less fearful of "the devil under every rock," and more trusting, courageous, undeterred, and proactive in the face of adversity as they built the world's largest Christian family of networks.

Central to Brother Billheimer's core theology is the fact that "the cross is the true center of history," and without it virtually nothing else in our lives makes any sense. Almost all believers would agree that the cross is where our power and authority on this earth come from. Even so, many things in our lives are difficult to understand, and we often face circumstances in which it hardly feels like God is in control or that Jesus truly was "victorious" over the enemy.

As you'll read in the following pages, Brother Billheimer offers an amazing insight into the heart of God, helping all followers of Jesus bring into focus the truth that what happens in our relatively short lives is in reality "on the job training for eternity." For as difficult as some things are, the question remains: how do you know you have faith unless it's called upon?

For some, this may seem a radical departure from personal experience, but Laurie and I can attest firsthand that it is a biblical truth that resonates in the heart of God. In fact, a few years ago, Laurie had a life-changing experience that more than confirmed what Paul Billheimer taught us. She was sitting in a very busy restaurant when everything around her seemed to dim and she felt like she was suddenly with the Lord. In a deeply loving and reassuring voice, He asked her one simple question: "What do you have to bring Me?"

Of course, all Laurie could think was, "What could I have that would be of any value to the Creator of heaven and earth?" Before she could respond, her entire life began flashing before her eyes like a video. Curiously, there were large gaps in the events, as if whole chunks of the tape of her life had been erased. Those moments that did play out were all scenes of painful hardship, sickness, and difficulty. Yet they clearly weren't all the trials and tribulations she'd faced in her life, leaving her wondering what had happened to all the rest.

And then she realized the fullness of what she was seeing. The events God was showing her were only those agonizing situations in which, rather than embracing worry or despair, she had stood fast in the Lord, declaring the truth of who God is and His intentions for her in the midst of her troubles. All the "blank spaces" were those trials and tribulations where she hadn't, where she had allowed her circumstances to dictate who she was, how she felt, and what she believed.

In other words, God was showing her that the only moments of our lives that get "recorded" in heaven — the only times that matter — are the times we choose to live by faith. Everything else is wasted time, not damning evidence God is storing up to use against us, but events God simply erases from existence, burying them "in the deepest part of the sea and remembering them no more."

As the "video" of her life ended and Laurie found herself sitting back in the busy restaurant again, she was left with a profound revelation and an answer to the question God had asked her: "What do you have to bring Me?"

Rather than explain any further, I'll leave it to Brother Billheimer to escort you on your own journey into understanding the purposes and intentions of God. If Laurie's experience helps illuminate the "what," then this book lays out the "why" — why a life of faith matters and why Jesus tells us that "in this life you will have tribulations...."

We can confidently assert that the profound truths found in *Destined for the Throne* are as relevant today as they were when it was first published a generation ago, perhaps more, given the times we live in. That's why we're excited to release a new edition of this life-changing book. As it did when my parents first discovered it all those years ago, we believe that it is going to impact a new generation of God's people to walk in confident faith and victory as they follow Him wholeheartedly.

May God richly bless you as you discover that you really are — DESTINED FOR THE THRONE!

Matt and Laurie Crouch

Trinity Broadcasting Network

# Destined for the Throne

---

## How Reigning in Life Now
### Prepares Us to Reign With Christ in Eternity

This special edition for

## Trinity Broadcasting Network

P.O. Box 316
Ft. Worth, Texas 76161

Toll free prayer line (U.S. and Canada): 1-888-731-1000
International:  +1-714-731-1000
www.tbn.org

"And they sang a new song, saying:

'You are worthy to take the scroll,

And to open its seals;

For You were slain,

And have redeemed us to God by Your blood

Out of every tribe and tongue and people and nation,

And have made us kings and priests to our God;

And we shall reign on the earth.'"

– REVELATION 5:9-10 [NKJV]

# Destined for the Throne

## How Reigning in Life Now
Prepares Us to Reign With Christ in Eternity

### PAUL E. BILLHEIMER

A STUDY IN BIBLICAL COSMOLOGY
setting forth
THE ULTIMATE GOAL OF THE UNIVERSE
which is
THE CHURCH REIGNING WITH CHRIST
with a New View of PRAYER as
"ON-THE-JOB" TRAINING IN PREPARATION
for THE THRONE

**Trilogy Christian Publishers**

This edition published by:

**Trilogy Christian Publishers**
A Wholly Owned Subsidiary of
Trinity Broadcasting Network
P.O. Box 316
Ft. Worth, Texas 76161

**ISBN: 978-1-64088-996-5** (Print)

**ISBN: 978-1-64088-997-2** (E-book)

Printed in the United States of America

## Dedicated to My Wife
## Jenny E. Billheimer

For her valuable assistance, not only in transcribing the manuscript, but also in offering valid criticism and appropriate suggestions, this little volume is affectionately dedicated.

## CHAPTER NUMBER 7 *(Continued)*

## CHAPTER NUMBER 8

### The Problem of Faith

## CHAPTER NUMBER 9

### Organized Action

## PERSONAL JOURNAL

## (Important)

It's impossible to find a system of philosophy or theology that someone hasn't questioned or disputed. Two competing views of theology, Calvinism and Arminianism, are good examples of this. Each has its sincere defenders as well as its equally sincere opponents. Yet each has a large number of supporters who believe its unique theological system is the true and reasonable one with much to back it up.

In the area of philosophy, the science of reasoning, it seems no one school of thought gives a satisfying explanation of the universe. All fall a little short of presenting a clear cause or source to help us understand the reason and the meaning of existence. Science, with all it does to enrich and ease lives, does not offer much help here. No, we must go to the Bible for this kind of wisdom; without help from the Bible, the universe remains a puzzle, a mystery that cannot be understood. Only the Bible offers answers that make sense to these age-old questions: Who is man? Why is he here? What is the meaning of life?

At first, many of the insights and principles discussed in the pages of this book seemed so out of the ordinary, so amazing to me that they staggered my imagination and boggled my mind. I wouldn't be surprised if the reader finds some of the concepts just as startling. For this reason, I urge the reader to carefully look at the ideas presented here in the light of both Scripture and logic.

I can say that wherever messages taken from the contents of this book have been given, whether in a sermon or in a personal conversation, they have been received with appreciation. I believe the following pages contain a message especially relevant to this end time. This book is offered to the Church with my sincere prayer that it will become a useful and important gift to the spiritual life of the Body and Bride of Christ.

I deeply feel that the personal ministry of the Holy Spirit through the Word of God gave to me many of the insights written on these pages. Because of this, I freely give up all claim of ownership. My desire is that my ministerial brothers will feel perfectly free to use, in their own ministry, any material in this book which the Spirit may make meaningful to them, subject only to the terms of the copyright. The truths were given by the Spirit. They belong to the Body.

**Paul E. Billheimer**

# Foreword by Billy Graham

I have just read the manuscript of Paul E. Billheimer's book *Destined for the Throne*, and have been inspired and challenged by the insights and fresh interpretations of the Scriptures regarding prayer, praise and the Church's place in the world. Every Christian who feels impelled to find a deeper dimension of Christian witness should not only read this book, but also study it prayerfully, and apply its principles to his life.

**Billy Graham**

The following chapters present what some consider a totally new and unique Christian cosmology or understanding of the universe. My main point is this: the one purpose of the universe from all eternity is the creation and preparation of an Eternal Companion for God's Son, called the Bride, the Lamb's Wife. Since the Bride is to share the throne of the entire universe with her Divine Lover and Lord as a "judicial equal," she must be trained, educated and made ready for her queenly role.

Because the crown is only for those who win the battle (Rev. 3:21), the Church (later to become the Bride) must learn the art of spiritual warfare, of defeating evil forces, in order to sit with her Lord on His throne after the Marriage Supper of the Lamb. To help her gain the skill of winning in spiritual battle, God chose the wise program of believing prayer. He did not choose prayer mainly as a way of getting things done. It is His way of giving the Church on-the-job training in overcoming the forces lined up against God. This world is like a great laboratory where those destined for the throne are learning through actual practice how to win against Satan and his demons. The place of prayer is the place of action, the arena where overcomers are produced.

This means that *redeemed humanity* — those who love and follow Christ — outranks all other levels of created beings in the universe. Angels are created, not generated. Redeemed humanity is both created and generated, born of God, bearing His genes, renewed by His heredity. Through this new birth a redeemed human being becomes a true member of the original cosmic family, "next of kin" to the Trinity. In other words, God has raised redeemed humanity — born again Christians — to such a heavenly height that it is impossible for Him to lift them up further without offending the Godhead. This is the basis for the strong praise of Psalm 8:5: "Yet you made them only a little lower than God and crowned them with glory and honor" (NLT).

The Church, by identifying with the resurrection and ascension of Christ, is already legally on the throne. Through the use of her weapons of prayer and faith she holds in this present throbbing moment the balance of power in world affairs. In spite of all of her sad weaknesses, shocking failures, and inexcusable sins, the Church is still the greatest force for civilization and enlightened social consciousness in the world today. The only force that is fighting against Satan's total rule in human affairs is the Church of the Living God.

If no one stood against Satan, if he were not held back by the Spirit-led prayers and holy lives of God's people, "the pillared firmament itself were rottenness and earth's base built on stubble" (Alexander Maclaren). "You are the salt of the earth....You are the light of the world" (Matt. 5:13-14, NLT). If it were not for the cleansing and keeping power of the Church on the earth, the framework of all we call civilization would totally fall apart, decay and disappear. The fact that the social order has been kept intact and not completely destroyed in spite of Satan's most evil acts, proves that at least a part of the Church is operating as it should and has already begun to share rulership with her Lord. She is, even now, because of her weapons of prayer and faith, involved in on-the-job training for her place as co-ruler with Christ over the whole universe, following Satan's final destruction.

The Church, by her constant use of prayer, holds the balance of power not only in world affairs but also in the salvation of individual souls. Without going against the free moral choice and responsibility of any person, the Church, by using constant, believing prayer, can help release the power of the Holy Spirit on that person. The Spirit's influence causes him or her to find it easier to give in to the Spirit's tender call and be saved than to continue in hardness of heart.

God will not go over the Church's head to do things in spite of her because this would work against His plan to bring her to the full maturity she needs to become co-ruler with the Son. Because of this, God will do nothing without her. John Wesley agrees with this when he says, "God does nothing but in answer to prayer."

In order to prepare the Church to overcome Satan, God entered the stream of human history in the Incarnation. As a sinless, perfect Man He overcame and destroyed Satan both legally and literally. All that Christ did in redemption He did for the good of the Church. He is "head over all things to the church" (Eph. 1:22). His victory over Satan is assigned *to the Church*. Although Christ's triumph over Satan is full and complete, God allows him to carry on guerrilla warfare. God could put away Satan completely, but He has chosen to use him to give the Church on-the-job training in spiritual warfare.

Prayer is not begging God to do something He doesn't want to do. It is not an effort to make God willing to act. Prayer is enforcing Christ's victory over Satan. It is carrying out, on earth, decisions already made in Heaven concerning the affairs of men. The cross of Calvary legally destroyed Satan and erased all of his claims. God put the carrying out of Calvary's victory in the hands of the Church (Matt. 18:18 and Luke 10:17-19). He has given to her power of attorney. She is His representative. This given authority works only through the prayers of a believing Church. Therefore, *prayer is where the action is*. Any church without a well-organized and systematic prayer program is simply operating a religious treadmill.

Further, we can be sure if prayer does not get answered, it is because strong faith is missing. If our faith is not strong and victorious, it is because praise is missing — *ongoing, powerful and directed praise*. Praise is the highest form of prayer because it puts our requests together with faith. Praise is the spark plug of faith. It is the one thing we need to get our faith up and going, helping it rise above the heavy fog of our doubts. Praise is the soap that cleanses our faith and washes away any doubt from our heart. The secret of answered prayer is faith without doubt (Mark 11:23). And the secret of faith without doubt is praise — powerful praise, ongoing praise, praise that is a way of life. This kind of praise is the answer to a living, dynamic faith and prayer that gets results.

The secret of success in overcoming Satan, and qualifying for the throne is a huge program of practical, productive prayer. The secret of productive prayer is a massive program of praise.

These and other principles of prayer are discussed and expanded in the pages of this book.

# 1

# The Ultimate Goal of the Universe: The Church

## God Is the Lord of History

Today, few experts on human history have any idea of its true meaning and purpose. They may be able to organize and systematize all the events and personalities that make up history's raw material, but they don't have a clue about the significance of the things they record. Some historians actually admit this. G. N. Clark, giving his inaugural address at Cambridge, said, "There is no secret and no plan in history to be discovered." French novelist, André Maurois, presumes, "The universe is indifferent. Who created it? Why are we here on this puny mud heap spinning in infinite space? I have not the slightest idea, and I am quite convinced no one has . . . ." Other experts aren't so blunt but are just as confused about the purpose of events and the motive of the characters about whom they write. It has not entered their minds that God is actually in control of history.

## Ancient Thinkers Puzzled Over Our Existence

The ancient Greeks thought about history as a circle or a cycle, always repeating itself and going nowhere in particular. To them our very existence was a mystery that could never be understood, and this appears to be the same reasoning of many modern, secular historians. They do not know what existence is all about. To them, and much of our world, history is simply one senseless crisis after another and has no purpose, rhyme, or reason. They cannot give a rationale for intelligent life or the existence of the human race. To them, no answer concerning where we came from or where we are going can be found. All "being" is just a huge, confusing puzzle. Their view of history is bewildering, frustrating and hopeless.

## Modern Thinkers Say the Universe Has No Purpose

This philosophy of meaninglessness was made popular by Frenchman Jean-Paul Sartre, who taught that each person exists in a watertight container as a detached individual in an aimless universe. He said since we can't know who we are or where we came from or where we are going; since we don't understand the past and have no hope of the future, then the present throbbing moment is all that counts. Only the present has meaning. Long-term goals are not important. Therefore, to sacrifice something in the present for the future is stupid. Out of Sartre's teaching came the "now generation," the generation which cannot wait for anything. They believe the only reason we exist is for the pleasure of the moment. Their motto is "On with the dance, let joy be unconfined." The apostle Paul described the attitude of those who had no hope for the future: "Let us eat and drink; for tomorrow we die" (1 Cor. 15:32).

In the 1960's this outlook on life created a generation of college youth full of themselves. Since they felt free to do exactly as they pleased, never answering to anyone, and held no hope for the future, their lives became marked by emptiness and depression. An eruption of revolutionary violence, arson and theft spread death and destruction in cities and on college campuses around the world. Almost overnight, society exploded in crime, rioting, murder, and in the insanity of the drug culture. All this was the result of a worldview marked by ignorance about the past and hopelessness concerning the future.[1]

## The Bible Is the Only Infallible Source Book

The average expert on things historical has no clue about the meaning of history because he ignores the only infallible source book — the Bible. Christians, those who claim to be followers of Christ, hold the Bible to be the only sacred Book in the world given to human beings by direct communication from God. That Book alone contains the truth and purpose about human life on earth. Yet, for most people, including the writers of history in our day, the center of history for any specific period of time is the largest country, with the most people, greatest wealth, and most powerful army. To most of us, the stuff of history is the part played by the great empires of the past led by bigger than life leaders like the Pharaohs of Egypt, Alexander the Great of Greece, the Caesars of Rome, or Napoleon of France — these seem to be the true history makers. Empire builders like these believed they were the center of the universe, the ultimate "movers and shakers" of history and its events.

## The Cross Is the True Center of History

The world and its experts have failed to recognize the cross as the true center of history. Only one view of history makes sense, and it is the story told by the Bible.[2]

The center of history is neither its great empires (Egypt, Babylon, Greece, or Rome), nor their modern counterparts (Russia, China, the United States, or in any other nation that may try to take center stage). No, to find the center of history, we must travel past all these vast empires and their powerful leaders and find our way to a tiny land called the "navel of the world," literally the center of the earth, Israel. In that tiny land we must discover a tiny hill called Mount Calvary where, 2,000 years ago, a Man named Jesus was nailed to a cross and lifted up to die. Yes, that Man on that cross on that tiny hill in that tiny land is the true center of all history of this world as well as the myriad of galaxies and island universes in outer space from here to eternity.

## The Church, God's "Eternal Companion," Is the Goal of History

The cross is the center of history, and the Church is the goal of history. Why? The Man hanging on that bloody cross, mocked and humiliated by onlookers, existed "before all things" (Col. 1:17). He existed before history itself. In fact, He is the starting point of our history, for "all things were made by him; and without him was not anything made that was made" (John 1:3). The history He put in motion is also shaped and controlled by Him. "He regulates the universe by the mighty power of his command" (Heb.1:3, TLB). As He "regulates" the universe, this Man Jesus has a single, specific purpose, which is the central and controlling factor of history, no matter how wide its sweep may be.

Every event in history happens to serve that purpose. Nothing, no matter how small, is left out of the scheme of things. The universe, including this planet, was created for the one purpose of providing a suitable home for the human race[3], the object of this Man's affection. Humankind was created in the very image and likeness of God to fulfill one *goal*: to fashion a composite "Eternal Companion" for the Son of God, Jesus.

After man's fall, his failure to obey God in the Garden of Eden, God made a promise to redeem him and put him back on track through the future Messiah or "Anointed One." God carefully chose the Messianic ancestry who would bring in the Messiah. The Messiah came with only one intention: to give birth to His Church, the "called out ones," the ones who would be restored to that perfect God-like image. These would collectively become His Bride. It follows that the Church, the called out and redeemed, turns out to be the focus and goal of all history, of all that God has been doing in all kingdoms and dimensions, whether earthly or heavenly, for all eternity.

If this is true, then ALL history is sacred. There is no such thing as secular, mundane or common history. If this is true, then history is simply "HIS STORY." The whole universe is working with God in His purpose to choose and prepare the Church as His Son's Eternal Companion. The entire cosmos is organized for this purpose because all things belong to the Church and are for her benefit (1 Cor. 3:21-23). As the *Lord of History*, God is controlling all of its events, not only on earth but in heaven, to bring His Bride to maturity, beauty, perfection, and, finally, to the throne beside His Son. God is not preparing angels or archangels for this purpose, but the Church, His chosen Bride[4]. The apostle Paul writes about this: "We know that all things [the entire cosmos] work together [are cooperating] for good to them that love God [the Church], to them who are the called according to His purpose [the Bride]" (Rom. 8:28).

## Romance Lives at the Heart of the Universe

Yes, romance lives at the heart of the universe. It is the key to all existence, all "being." Even from eternity God purposed that there should be a Bride in His Son's future, a Companion worthy to sit with Him on His throne. John the Revelator describes her as "the bride, the Lamb's wife" (Rev. 21:9). John also tells us that she will share the Bridegroom's throne (Rev. 3:21) following the "Marriage Supper of the Lamb." This is the ultimate purpose, the climactic goal of history.

We see in Romans 8:28 that this is the one and only reason behind all of God's creative acts. Everything God has been doing from the beginning has been focused on the Church. This fact alone sheds light on our history and helps us understand it[5]. No ordinary, secular historian can be expected to comprehend this. But, if we truly understand Romans 8:28, then it is for the Church that suns and moons wax and wane; for her starry galaxies fill the heavens; for her, island universes swing in outer space; for her, all earthly kingdoms rise and fall (Psalm 75:6-7 and Psalm 105).

It follows that powerful leaders like Pharaoh, Nebuchadnezzar, Darius, Sennacherib, and others were not raised up because of their own importance. This is the message of Isaiah 10:5-14 [TLB]. No, these kings were only significant because of their relationship to God's purpose for the Messianic nation, through whom Messiah would come. One day we will understand that not only these Biblically recorded happenings but also all events from all eternity were set in place for one purpose: the eventual winning and preparation of the Bride.

In his *Bible Handbook* (New Revised Edition, Page 20), Henry Halley has pointed out that " ... the Old Testament is the account of a nation. The New Testament is the account of a MAN. The Nation was founded and nurtured of God to bring the Man into the world." What was the purpose of the Man? He came to die — to die and rise again (John 12:27). What was the purpose of that? The usual response is that He died and rose again to save the world.

## God's Salvation Is for Everyone, But Not Everyone Receives It

Is this answer too simplistic? Does it fail to include all the factors involved? It is true that Christ's death and rising from the dead did provide redemption for *all* mankind. Not one person of the human race was left out. "He is the sacrifice for our sins. He takes away not only our sins, but the sins of *all the world*" (1 John 2:2, NLT). God includes everyone who has ever been born, from the beginning of human history to its end, in His all-inclusive, redemptive love. But, God knew from the very start that only a relatively small number of people would accept His universal offer. Jesus put it this way in Matthew 7:13-14: "You can enter God's Kingdom only through the narrow gate. The highway to hell is broad, and its gate is wide for the many who choose that way. But the gateway to life is very narrow and the road is difficult, and only a few ever find it" (NLT).

It stands to reason if God knew from the beginning only a few, a tiny minority comparatively speaking, would respond to all of His creative activity, including the plan of redemption, that small group would become the "apple of His eye." He would focus all of His plans, purposes and creative actions on them[6]. *Therefore, it follows that it was for the sake of this small group that the universe was created in the first place.* It was for them the inhabitants of outer space, the unseen world of angelic beings, were brought into being (Heb. 1:14). It was for them this planet was formed. For their sake, the human race was born. In order to make them His very own, God Himself entered the stream of human history in the Incarnation — God became flesh. This small group is called the Church, the Bride, the Lamb's Wife (Matt. 16:18, Rev. 21:9).[7]

## The Bride Is God's Masterpiece of All Time

How can we be sure this is true? How can we be sure the Bride is really the divine focus of the Creator of the Universe? Let's look at what is called "the residual argument."[8] If a person wants to know the meaning and purpose of history, he must look at the end, the final outcome. How can we do this? Remember, the Bible is the believer's ultimate Source Book. Since Biblical prophecy is history written in advance, we have history's final chapter in the Book of Revelation. Look at the closing pages. One thing alone emerges as the final Masterpiece of the ages: *the Eternal Companion of the God-Man.* The final outcome and goal of events from eternity to eternity, the finished product of all the ages, is the shining, spotless Bride of Christ. She is joined with Him in marital joy at the Marriage Supper of the Lamb and seated with her heavenly Bridegroom on the throne of the universe — ruling and reigning with Him over an ever increasing and expanding Kingdom. Christ (Messiah) came to earth as a man for this one purpose: to claim His Beloved (Rev. 19:6-9; 21:1, 7, 9-10).

*Therefore, the Church, and only the Church, is the key to understanding history.* The Church — blood-washed, cleansed and gleaming in her white robes — is the center, the reason, and the goal of all of God's awesome handiwork. History, then, is only the servant of the Church, and the nations of the world are merely puppets in God's hands to carry out His purposes for His Church (Acts 17:26). *Creation has no other aim. History has no other goal.* From the beginning of time to the dawn of eternal ages, God has been working toward one awe-inspiring event, one majestic climax of history — the glorious wedding of His Son, the Marriage Supper of the Lamb.

## The Heavenly Wedding Is the Beginning of God's Eternal Plan

To grasp the meaning of God's design in all this, we need

to look back at Adam and Eve in the Garden of Eden. God saw that it was not good for Adam to be alone and He created a partner who was just right for him; he named her Eve. God also saw that it was not good for His Son to be alone. From the very beginning, it was God's plan and purpose that out of the wounded side of His Son Jesus should come an Eternal Companion to sit by His side on the throne of the universe. She would be a true partner, a "judicial equal,"⁹ to share in His sovereign power and authority over His eternal kingdom. Listen to Jesus' own words in Luke 12:32, "Fear not, little flock, for it is your Father's good pleasure to give you the kingdom." And in Rev. 3:21 the Lord tells us, "Those who are victorious will sit with me on my throne, just as I was victorious and sat with my Father on his throne" (NLT).

It is clear that to be given the kingdom is more than taking to heart kingdom standards and values; that would only be one phase of it. To be given the kingdom is to be made a *king*, to be given authority over a kingdom. The apostle Paul confirms this is what God had in mind for the Church in 1 Corinthians 6:2-3: "Don't you know that someday we Christians are going to judge and govern the world? . . . Don't you realize that we Christians will judge and reward the very angels in heaven?" (TLB). This is just a down payment on what Jesus meant when He said, "I have given them the glory you gave me" (John 17:22, NLT).

This promotion to royalty and rulership is not a hollow, empty or symbolic thing. It is not an imaginary promise. The Church, the Bride, the Eternal Companion of God's Son is to sit *with Him* on His throne. If His throne represents reality, then her throne is no fantasy. Neither "joint heir" can do anything alone. "The Spirit Himself bears witness with our spirit that we are children of God, and if children, then heirs — heirs of God and joint heirs with Christ, if indeed we suffer with [Him], that we may also be glorified together" (Romans 8:16-17, NKJV).

We may not know why it pleases the Father to give the kingdom to His "little flock." We may not know why Christ chooses to share His throne and His glory with the redeemed people who love and follow Him. We only know that He *has chosen* to do so and that it gives Him pleasure.

In light of all this, it is clear that everything that comes before the Marriage Supper of the Lamb is basic and in preparation of things to come. Only afterwards will God's eternal program begin to come to light and make sense. God will not be ready, so-to-speak, to launch His greatest enterprise of the ages until the Bride is on the throne next to her divine Lover and Lord. Until then, the whole universe is under the Son's control, and God is arranging everything for one purpose — to prepare and train the Bride for her eternal role. Truly, God is the Lord of history.

# NOTES

1. This worldview of disregard for the past and gloom about the future is repeated in the view of some biologists. In his book *Chance and Necessity,* Jacques Monod, the French molecular biologist, argues that man's existence is due to the chance meeting between tiny pieces of nucleic acid (genetic code) and proteins in the vast "pre-biotic soup." According to Dr. Francis Schaeffer's quotation of Monod in his book, *Back to Freedom and Dignity,* Monod believes that "all life results from interaction of pure chance — and necessity." Monod concludes that man is alone (as far as a Superior Being is concerned) in a huge universe, which he entered only by chance. There is no place to go to find his true destiny or even his duty as a human being. As Dr. Schaeffer states it in his book, Monod is sure that "man is the product of the impersonal, plus time, plus chance."

   If this is true, then man has no more value than any other part of the universe. There is no moral difference between cutting down a tree and destroying a human being. If a human being is truly no different from a tree, then his future is no different. Man's existence has no more meaning than the existence of a tree. His value is reduced to zero. The end result is meaninglessness and despair. According to Dr. Schaeffer, this is what triggered the 1960's student rebellion on college campuses throughout our nation and the world. When man destroys God, he destroys himself. *Atheism is suicidal.*

2. This viewpoint is expressed by Erich Sauer: "As the Creator of the course of history and Governor of heaven and earth He [God] controls the universal process. Therefore, as the Lord of history, He and He alone, can explain history . . . .Therefore, the Bible is the 'Book of mankind' — the key to world events. All understanding to the whole of human affairs depends upon the attitude to it" (*From Eternity to Eternity,* page 97). "All history is incomprehensible without Christ" (Ernest Renan).

3. All traditional discussion agrees that the Bible's description of creation pictures man as the finishing touch of the creation

# NOTES

process. Even Nietzsche said, "Man is the reason for the world" (Erich Sauer in *The King of the Earth,* page 49).

Leonard Verduin says this about the story of creation in the book of Genesis: "The plain implication is that from the earliest beginnings the divine interest was to reach its climax in man. All that goes before is anticipatory, propaedeutic (introductory) to man. Man is pictured as the crown and capstone of the entire creative enterprise of the Almighty; man is the goal toward which the whole undertaking moved. Verily, the Bible does not speak meanly (poorly, unsatisfactorily) of man" (*Somewhat Less Than God,* Page 9).

Watchman Nee points out that the Church is now the body of Christ, but will be His Bride after the Marriage Supper of the Lamb (*The Glorious Church,* Chapter 3, page 46, 1968 edition).

4.  The opinion of this section has been challenged on the ground "that too much is being built on one verse out of context."

    I recognize this criticism makes sense because the word translated "all things" in Romans 8:28 is not the word used for the cosmos (creation) elsewhere.

    However, consider this: if *some* events are working for the good of the Church then *all events in the entire universe* must also be working for her good; this is a necessary conclusion of the doctrine of monotheism — the belief that there is only one God.

    If there is only one God and He is supreme, then all of His purposes and actions work together to accomplish the same thing. Only if there is a rival power or divided authority could there be cross currents or purposes; this would produce terrible confusion. Therefore, if there is one supreme God in the universe, then the universe is a "cosmos." If the universe is a cosmos — a harmonious and ordered whole — then all circumstances and events in the cosmos are working toward the same goal.

# NOTES

The notion that the Lord is totally in control is taught by Psalm 103:19: "The LORD has made the heavens his throne; from there he rules over everything" (NLT). This truth is the theme of many of the Psalms and Old Testament prophets and appears throughout all Scripture from Genesis to Revelation. This means the entire universe is one beautiful arrangement, logical and totally in harmony with itself — a cosmos.

In such a universe under the control of a central absolute authority (God), if one event or series of events is working for the good of the Church, then *all* events are serving the same purpose.

A clear example of the cosmos cooperating in God's Messianic purpose (the coming of Christ to earth), and therefore in His purpose for the Church, is found in Judges 5:20, "The stars in their courses fought against Sisera." Many other passages illustrate this same point.

*Therefore, the "all things" of Romans 8:28 includes not only certain limited facts and events, but the sum total of all that is contained in the universe.*

5. I believe that the redeemed — those who love and follow Christ — are too large a crowd to be counted (Rev. 7:9). The terms "small group" and "tiny minority" are used comparatively of those who freely chose or will choose to follow Christ down through the centuries. If the countless millions who died or will die as infants or in their mother's womb are included in the redeemed, as we believe, this saying may be true: "that ultimately the lost shall bear to the saved no greater proportion than the inmates of a prison do to the mass of the community."

6. I believe that the Church includes all the redeemed from creation to eternity.

7. The automobile industry gives us an eye-opening example of what has been termed "the residual argument." The automobile

# NOTES

was once but a concept, an idea, a dream in the mind of a man, but that idea gave rise to a great enterprise. To manufacture the automobile, huge structures covering thousands of acres of land have been built at great cost. These plants have been filled with highly advanced machines, tools, and equipment costing large sums of money. The whole process takes great amounts of raw materials of many kinds from around the world. These industrial complexes give work to millions of men and women from engineers to assembly line operators. All of this is for one reason and one alone: to produce a tiny automobile. When that first small vehicle comes from the assembly line, the purpose of this vast group of industries becomes perfectly clear. All that has gone before, including the huge cost, the processing of raw material with its resultant huge amounts of waste, everything from the drawing board to the last bolt is explained by one thing and one alone: the existence of a motor car. That small car is the key that unlocks the mystery of all the time and effort that came before it.

8.  Judicial — "allowed, enforced or set by order of a judge or law court" (*Webster's New World Dictionary*). The equality, which is in view here, is a "given" or assigned equality. Although it is a given equality, it is as *fully recognized and respected as if it were original or divine.* This delegated equality is unmistakably implied in the term "joint heir" (Rom. 8:17). In law, a joint heir can do nothing alone, nothing without the other.

# 2

# God's Purpose for the Church: Supreme Rank

## Supreme Rank of Redeemed Humanity

It must be clear from the previous chapter that redeemed humanity — those who have chosen to love and follow Christ — have been placed in a totally unique position in the universe's chain of command. This is not to demean angels or cast a shadow on their radiance and glory. No, they are beautiful beyond words, majestic, extremely powerful and supernaturally intelligent. Angels rule heavenly regions of uncharted vastness and unimaginable grandeur. Their obvious importance is confirmed by the fact that God has chosen them to surround His throne, to make up the court of the King of kings. Yet, as respected as they are, even the highest ranking angel hovering over God's throne is outranked — wonder of wonders — by the most insignificant human being who has been "born again," redeemed and restored by the blood of the Lamb.

## God Showed Us His Eternal Plan in the Incarnation

Humanity was created originally in the image of God. *Redeemed* humanity has been elevated by means of a *divinely conceived genetic process* (known as the "new birth") to the highest rank of all created beings. What does this mean? According to Hebrews 2:16, "For verily he [God] took not on him the nature of angels; but he took on him the seed of Abraham" (KJV). God could not become *incarnate* (become embodied) in angels because they were not created in the full image of God.[1] No other created being was given the capacity of the human being to "contain and utter (express) God." Only man has a nature in which God can become incarnate — take on bodily form, or "become flesh" (John 1:14). So, God "tipped His hand," so-to-speak, in the Incarnation. By coming to earth in the form of a man, He showed us His plan. By the Incarnation, God dignified the human race and raised up redeemed humanity beyond even the highest-ranking angel in all of heaven.

## Angels Created — Not Generated

Because angels were not made in the image and likeness of God, He could not become incarnate in them, and fallen angels cannot be redeemed. No angel can ever become a natural member of the family of God. No angel can become a blood-born son of God. Angels can never have the heritage, the genes of God. They can never have a part in the divine nature (2 Peter 1:4). Neither can angels become members of the corporate Bride of Christ. These privileges are reserved for redeemed human beings alone.

We cannot imagine an angel saying, "See how very much our Father loves us, for he calls us his children, and that is what we are!" Neither can we think of an angel telling us, "But we do know that we will be like him, for we will see him as he really is" (1 John 3:1-2, NLT). Another scripture confirms that only the redeemed have the privilege of sonship, Hebrews 2:11: "So now Jesus and the ones he makes holy have the same Father. That is why Jesus is not ashamed to call them his brothers and sisters" (NLT). Further, to which of the angels has God said at any time, "You are my brother or sister or mother"? that is, "We are all of one origin, we have been birthed by the same Father" (Matt. 12:48-50)? Did He ever say of the angels as He said of His disciples, "that they all may be one, as You, Father, [are] in Me, and I in You; that they also may be one in Us ... that they may be one just as We are one: I in them, and You in Me; that they may be made perfect in one ... " (John 17:21-23, NKJV)? Did Paul ever say of the angels as he did of the Church, that they make up His Body of which He is the Head, "the fullness of Him who fills all in all" (Eph. 1:23, NKJV)? Did Paul say to angels, or to the Church, "For we are members of His body, of His flesh and of His bones" (Eph. 5:30, NKJV)?

## The Redeemed Are Part of God's Family, an "Extension" of the Godhead

But this is not all. We walk softly here. With bated breath we read in 1 Corinthians 6:17: "He that is joined to the Lord is one spirit." This union goes beyond a mere formal or idealistic harmony or rapport. It is an *organic* (living) unity, an "organic relationship of personalities" (Sauer). Through the new birth we become actual members of the original cosmic family (Eph. 3:15), true sons of God (1 John 3:2), "partakers of the divine nature" (2 Peter 1:4), produced by Him, infused with His genes (No physical relationship is implied), called the seed or "sperma" of God (1 John 5:1, 18 and 1 Peter 1:3, 23), and carrying His heredity. Through the new birth — and I speak reverently — we become the "next of kin" to the Trinity, a kind of "extension" of the Godhead — Father, Son and Holy Spirit. Yes, this group of redeemed humanity outranks all other orders of created beings. Paul emphasizes this point with his dramatic questions in 1 Corinthians 6:2-3: "Don't you know that some day we Christians are going to judge and govern the world?...Don't you realize that we Christians will judge and reward the very angels in heaven?" (TLB)

## The New Species

Here is a completely new, unique, and exclusive breed of beings, which may be called a "new species." *There is nothing like it in all the eternal kingdoms.* This is the order of beings, which God had in mind when He spoke the worlds into existence. This is the order of beings, which Paul called "the new man" (Eph. 2:15), the "new humanity" destined through the new birth to become the royalty of the universe. They form a new ruling class who will make up the Bride, the Lamb's wife. This order is divinely chosen to be co-ruler, co-sovereign, co-administrator, and a judicially (see Chap. 1, Note 9) equal partner to the throne by the process of redemption and marriage to the King of kings.

## A Natural Family Circle

Be assured that nothing can ever change the fact that an infinite gulf separates the Creator God from His created children. Christ is the only eternally unique and only "begotten" Son, "the brightness of [God's] glory," and "the express image of his person" (Heb. 1:3.) From all eternity God purposed in His heart to have a family circle of His *very own*, not only created but *also given life* by His own life, including His own seed, genes or heredity. "Long ago, even before he made the world, God chose us to be *his very own* [in a genetic sense], through what Christ would do for us" (Eph. 1:4; also 5:25-27, 32, TLB). In order to bring about this personal, living family relationship, God put together the extremely wise plan of creation *plus* redemption through the new birth.

This concept would make it possible to bring "many sons to glory" (Heb. 2:10). "For from the very beginning God decided that those who came to him ... should become like his Son so that his Son would be the First, with many brothers" (Rom. 8:29, TLB). In other words, Christ is the Prototype (the Model). All other sons are to look just like Him. In John 1:12-13, we learn that the plan of redemption was put into motion to set up *a unique and productive method* by which these "many sons" would be born and then trained and set apart in such a way as to bring them into eternal glory. "But to all who believed him and accepted him, he gave the right to become children of God. They are reborn — not with a physical birth resulting from human passion or plan, but a birth that comes from God" (John 1:12-13, NLT). *Here is a distinct reference to two parallel generative (productive) methods, one human and the other divine.* Only through Christ can God the Father fulfill His fatherly longing for a true family relationship. *Without this plan, God's family relationship would have been forever limited to the Trinity.*

## Princes of the Realm

If you have ever worked on an assembly line, you know that

a model has to be designed first. This model must be made and then tested before it is handed over to the assembly line. The purpose of the assembly line is to produce exact duplicates, perfect copies, of the original model. This is also God's purpose in the plan of redemption — to produce, by means of the new birth, an entirely new and unique species of human beings, exact copies of His Son. He plans to share with this new breed both His glory and His dominion; they will form a group of royal sons and daughters who become the governing and administrative staff of His eternal kingdom.

We must and do recognize the infinite distinction between the Eternal Son and the "many sons" born into the family. Yet, because of the new birth, God recognizes their heredity as true blood brothers. And, according to 1 John 3:2, that is just what they are, true genetic sons of God and therefore blood brothers of the Son of God. Christ is the divine Model, and the new species will be made to look like Him. They are to be exact copies of Him, *as completely like Him as it is possible for the finite (limited) to be like the infinite (unlimited).*

As sons of God, birthed by Him, having in their very being and nature the genes (DNA) of God, they rank above all other created beings. God has raised them up to the most heavenly height possible, just short of becoming part of the Trinity itself. Although Christ is the unique and only begotten Eternal Son, yet *He does not keep His glory for Himself alone* for He has announced, "I have given them the glory you gave me" (John 17:22, NLT). Christ has made it possible for His redeemed people to share His glory and His rulership as truly responsible "Princes of the Realm."

# "Only a Little Lower than God" (Psalm 8:5, NLT)

God has raised up redeemed human beings to such an amazing height that it is impossible for Him to raise them any further without actually bringing them into the inner circle of the Godhead (Father, Son and Holy Spirit) itself. In our Beloved (Christ) we have been accepted into the very heart of the Father (John 1:18), and, because we are united with Christ, we are accepted on the same terms as He is accepted (Eph.1:6 and John 17:23). We are genuine sons of God, born again by the life of God Himself. We are full blood brothers of the Eternal Son. We are members of His Body of which He is the Head. We are spirit of His Spirit. How can we ever be brought closer? Rees Howells has beautifully expressed this mystery:

**So nigh, so very nigh to God, I cannot nearer be;**
**For in the Person of His Son, I am as near as He.**

These words agree with Psalm 8:4-5: "What is man, that thou art mindful of him? And the son of Man, that thou visitest him [in the Incarnation]? For thou has made him but little lower than God" (ASV). According to well-known scholars, this is the correct translation for the phrase, "little lower than God," since the term used for "God" in the original Hebrew is *Elohim*, the first of the names of deity (Gen. 1:1).

# Not Megalomania (Illusions of Grandeur/Greatness)

This all brings us to such dizzy heights that we may be

in danger of charges of megalomania, or of hyperbole (intentional exaggeration), or even blasphemy (assuming the rights or qualities of God) itself, if these conclusions are not true. *God has exhausted human language to open our eyes to the greatness of His plan for the redeemed.* Consider Paul's words in 1 Corinthians 2:9: "No eye has seen, no ear has heard, and no mind has imagined what God has prepared for those who love him" (NLT). Hallelujah!

So unbelievable is the hugeness of God's plan that Paul feels forced to pray strongly for us: "I pray that your hearts will be flooded with light so that you can see something of the future he has called you to share" (Eph. 1:18, TLB). Paul understood that we must have the help of the Holy Spirit to grasp even the beginning of the concept of becoming the next of kin to God Himself. Only faith inspired by the Holy Spirit can begin to understand the words of Psalm 8:5, "only a little lower than God."

## Not Fantasy

No, these words, these promises from God, are not fantasy. The natural mind may be overwhelmed by their true meaning, even tempted to say they are just make-believe, or perhaps symbols, or figures of speech. This is the way unbelief sometimes undermines the Word of God. Yet, one important rule of Biblical interpretation says the Word must be accepted as literal unless it is clearly figurative or symbolic. Even though the words "only a little lower than God" may be far beyond our ability to imagine, yet the words are true as far as our human mind can understand them. We must not rob the words of their meaning. They were meant to be accepted, not as fantasy, but literally, at face value. So, in God's eternal vocabulary, the rank or position of the redeemed is truthfully "only a little lower than God."

# Relationship Between Rank and Prayer

In light of all this, some might be wondering how this unusually close relationship with God affects the life of a Christian in regard to prayer and intercession. *The explanation is that prayer is not primarily God's way of getting things done. It is God's way of giving the Church on-the-job training in overcoming the forces hostile to God.* This world is a lab in which those destined for the throne are learning, by actual practice in prayer, how to overcome Satan and his demons. *God designed the program of prayer as an "apprenticeship" for eternal rulership with Christ.* Here we learn "the tricks of the trade" — how to use the weapons of prayer and faith in overcoming evil and enforcing Christ's victory. We don't know what enemies will be left to overcome in the world to come, but the character and strength gained in overcoming here on earth will evidently be needed when we join the Bridegroom on His throne. "To him who *overcomes* I will grant to sit with Me on My throne" (Rev. 3:21, NKJV). "The crown is only for the conqueror" (Sauer). The conqueror overcomes within the framework of God's program of prayer and faith. T*he place of prayer becomes the arena that produces the overcomer.*

# NOTES

1. Genesis 1:27 clearly suggests that sex, in its spiritual aspect, makes up a part of the image of God. "So God created man in His [own] image; in the image of God He created him; male and female He created them" (NKJV). If sex in its spiritual dimension is part of that image in which man was created, then it follows that angels were not created in the image of God — even though they may have other characteristics in common with man such as spirit nature; intellectual, emotional and moral gifts; and original holiness. See also Ephesians 5:22-32.

# 3

# The Mystery of Prayer

*"I looked for someone who might rebuild the wall of righteousness that guards the land. I searched for someone to stand in the gap in the wall so I wouldn't have to destroy the land, but I found no one. So now I will pour out my fury on them, consuming them with the fire of my anger. I will heap on their heads the full penalty for all their sins. I, the Sovereign LORD, have spoken!"* (Ezekiel 22:30-31, NLT)

## Prayer Is a Divine Mystery

Have you ever thought about prayer as a kind of puzzling mystery? Why is prayer even needed in God's management of things? Isn't He the Ruler of the universe and entirely self-sufficient? Could He possibly need any outside help? Isn't God all-powerful and all knowing? Why would He need to ask anything of man or any other creature? God spoke the stars and planets into being, and He keeps them in place by that same word. Can't He take care of everything without the help of puny man? "Of course!" you answer. Then, why did He even come up with the plan of prayer? Why and how did He become so dependent on the intercessions of people to carry out His purposes? Why did God box Himself in so that He can do nothing in the area of human redemption unless He has human help through

27

prayer and faith? How did He get Himself into such a fix? When God is totally self-sufficient — when He, by His own will and spoken word, can do anything — why doesn't He just go ahead, without caring about the opinions of man or any other intelligent being, and speak into being what He wants?

## God Is "Helpless" Without a Man

The words of the prophet Ezekiel shed some light on this mystery of prayer. During a time of national rebellion in Israel, God said, "I looked for someone who might rebuild the wall of righteousness that guards the land. I searched for someone to stand in the gap in the wall so I wouldn't have to destroy the land, but I found no one. So now I will pour out my fury on them, consuming them with the fire of my anger. I will heap on their heads the full penalty for all their sins. I, the Sovereign LORD, have spoken!" (Ezekiel 22:30-31, NLT).

Here we see that God wants to avoid punishing His unruly children. He longs to spare the nation of Israel. But, strangely, He is "helpless" without a man, without an intercessor to "stand in the gap." If no one will pray, God cannot withhold judgment. *Why?* Why should He be "dependent" on the prayers of a man to defend the people from judgments He Himself does not want to bring on them? God is the all-powerful Ruler of the universe. He is the ultimate Judge, Jury and Enforcement Authority. *Or is He?* If He longs to withhold judgment against His people, if He yearns to show mercy, why doesn't He just do it? Why doesn't He show mercy regardless of the prayers — or lack of prayers — of any man? Further, since God's will is supreme in all things, why doesn't He go ahead and carry out His purposes — like a person's salvation or a revival in a certain area? Why doesn't He go over our heads and make it happen? Why in the world would He set up a system that makes Him "dependent" on a person? This is truly an amazing mystery!

## God Begs Men to Pray

God's Word confirms this principle that He will do nothing in the area of human redemption outside of the strategy of prayer and intercession. We only need to look at His many compelling invitations to prayer. He not only invites us, He pleads with us. He insists. He urges. He even begs us to take part in this privilege. One translator has revised Matthew 7:7 like this: "Ask, I ask you to ask; seek, I entreat you to seek; knock, I urge you to knock." It seems clear that God can do nothing without our prayers.

Not only does He invite and encourage us to pray, He also commands us: "Ask the Lord of the harvest, therefore, to send out workers into his harvest field" (Matt. 9:38, NIV). God Himself is Lord of the harvest. The harvest is His. The laborers are His. *Why* should He stand "helplessly" by while pleading with men and women to pray for the workers needed in the fields? Why does He send out workers only in response to the prayers of His blood-bought children?

## God Absolutely Promises to Answer

God emphasizes the extreme importance of this plan of prayer by committing Himself positively—no holds barred—to answer. God's promises to answer prayer are so sweeping and over such a broad range, He might as well give out a "blank check" bearing His own signature. It is as though God is handing us His royal staff and begging us to use it. Here are some examples: "And I will do whatever you ask in my name, so that the Father may be glorified in the Son. You may ask me for anything in my name, and I will do it" (John 14:13-14, NIV). "But if you remain in me and my words remain in you, you may ask for anything you want, and it will be granted" (John 15:7, NLT)! "At that time you won't need to ask me for anything. I tell you the truth, you will ask the Father directly, and he will grant your request because you use my name. You haven't done this before. Ask, using my name, and you will receive, and you will have abundant joy" (John 16:23-24, NLT).

## His Plan of Prayer Is "Watertight"

I call these categorical promises, meaning they are unconditional. When I use that term I mean no attached conditions would prevent God from answering. In other words, all conditions are fair or reasonable for a true Christian. The condition of abiding (remaining, staying with) in Him and His words abiding in us is possible for any ordinary, sincere born-again believer. As Christians we want to stay in God's presence; we want His words to live inside us. If it isn't possible for true believers to do these things, then we would have to say God is hedging, that is, trying to avoid the risk involved in making such breathtaking promises — and that is impossible for Him. Now, if God is not hedging, then *the full responsibility for not praying, or for weak and useless prayer, falls on us!* If asking in the name of the Lord Jesus is not something any serious believer can do, then again, God is hedging. Yet, God is not hedging! He is doing business fairly. Therefore, the responsibility for not praying or for not receiving answers to our prayers is back in our court. The design of prayer, as far as God is concerned, is watertight. In fact, His part is already done. While His promise to answer is always marked off by His will, this is not a hedge, since any true child of God would not want anything but God's will. In other words, there is no fine print in God's prayer contract.

## God Makes the Decisions — His Church Carries Them Out

God's offer of His royal scepter to praying believers is a genuine offer. It is an offer in good faith. Through the plan of prayer God is actually inviting Christians into FULL partnership with Him, not in *making* the divine decisions, but in *carrying out* those decisions in the lives and activities of human beings. God makes the decisions governing the affairs of earth independently and by His own will. *The responsibility and authority for the enforcement and management of those decisions He has put on the shoulders of His Church.* "And I also say to you that you are Peter, and on this rock I will build My church, and the gates of Hades shall not prevail against it.[1] And I will give you the keys of the kingdom of heaven, and whatever you bind on earth will be bound in heaven, and whatever you loose on earth will be loosed in heaven" (Matt. 16:18-19, NKJV).

This promise is repeated to the Church in general in Matthew 18:18: "Assuredly, I say to you, whatever you bind on earth will be bound in heaven, and whatever you loose on earth will be loosed in heaven" (NKJV). Compare Luke 10:19:

"Behold, I give you the authority to trample on serpents and scorpions, and over all the power of the enemy, and nothing shall by any means hurt you" (NKJV). And, look at John 20:21-23: "Again Jesus said, 'Peace be with you! As the Father has sent me, I am sending you. And with that he breathed on them and said, 'Receive the Holy Spirit. If you forgive anyone's sins, their sins are forgiven; if you do not forgive them, they are not forgiven'" (NIV).

## God Makes the Church His Representative

As part of the Easter Sunday School lesson for April 14, 1968, Dr. Wilber T. Dayton commented on John 20:21-23: "After the removal of His bodily presence from among them, His followers must be His representatives, must take His place. This is the apostle's commission and ours. We are His proxies with power of attorney to do His bidding."

"As the Father has sent me, I am sending you" means what it says — the Lord sends us out as His representatives with full authority to carry out His will and His agenda. As His officers we are given the full power of the office of our Chief, and we are authorized to act in His place.

## Why?

By now, you are probably asking: *Why* did God choose to work within the boundaries of this plan of prayer? *Why* did He put the full burden of carrying out and managing His government of earth and its affairs on the shoulders of fallen but restored human beings? *Why* will He not do anything in world affairs without the aid of His Church? Most Protestants would reject the Roman Catholic idea that the Pope is God's vicegerent (representative) on earth. But, *haven't we failed to act on the enormous authority God has given to us, His Church, in the world?* Remember, that authority to carry out the will and decision of God regarding earthly activities and events only operates within the framework and plan of prayer, which God has chosen. By God's own order, this vast delegated authority has no power at all except through the prayers of believers (Ezekiel 20:30-31). What is the meaning of this plan? *Why* did God do it?

## Prayer Is a Privilege — The Badge of Rank

God had something wonderful in mind when He planned the system of prayer. Remember, God's eternal purpose in creating the universe and the human race was to obtain an Eternal Companion, a Bride, for His Son. This fact is a part of the mystery explained in the book of Ephesians, reaching its main point in chapter five. This chapter describes the parallel between God's human and divine marriage programs. Verse 32 clearly explains that the partners in the marriage program are Christ and His Church: "This is a great mystery, but it is an illustration of the way Christ and the church are one" (NLT).[2] In God's eternal plan the Church, as Christ's Eternal Companion, is to sit in the highest position in the whole universe just short of the Trinity itself. As the Bride of the Eternal Son, she will share with Him in universal rulership. Consider these Scriptures: "Don't you know that some day we Christians are going to judge and govern the world?...Don't you realize that we Christians will judge and reward the very angels in heaven?" (1 Cor. 6:2a, 3a, TLB). "If we suffer, we shall also reign with him" (2 Tim. 2:12). "To him who overcomes and does my will to the end, I will give authority [power] over the nations." (Rev. 2:26, NIV). "To him who overcomes, I will give the right to sit with me on my throne, just as I overcame and sat down with my Father on his throne" (Rev. 3:21, NIV). "And they sang a new song: 'You are worthy to take the scroll and to open its seals, because you were slain, and with your blood you purchased men for God from every tribe and language and people and nation. You have made them to be a kingdom and priests to serve our God, and they will reign on the earth" (Rev. 5:9-10, NIV).

*Redeemed members of the human race, the only race in all creation that was made in the image of God, will make up this Eternal Companion. Since this companion will share the throne of the universe with Christ, her Lover and Lord, she must be trained, educated and prepared for her queenly role.*

# Prayer Is "On-the-Job" Training for Rulership

God is preparing the Church for eternal rulership with Christ by giving her His power and authority to carry out His decisions and to enforce His will on the earth. By practicing this kind of enforcement of Heaven's decisions through prayer, the Church is actually in on-the-job training for her future royal position. She must learn the art of spiritual warfare, of overcoming evil forces, as she prepares for her succession to the throne after the Marriage Supper of the Lamb. *In order to help the Church learn how to overcome evil,*

*God came up with the plan of prayer. To give her on-the-job training, He gave her the authority to enforce His will right here on earth. In order to help her develop the character and the "know how" she will need as the Lord's Companion, God gave her both the responsibility and the authority to enforce His will and carry out His decisions on planet earth.*

Notice how often *earth*, as the place of action, is emphasized: "Whatever you bind on earth"; "Whatever you loose on *earth*"; "If two of you on *earth* agree about anything you ask for" (Matt. 16:19, Matt. 18:18-19, NIV). The Church has been given the greatest honor and the highest position of all created beings. That's because she has been given authority and administrative responsibility over earthly affairs. No angel or archangel will ever enjoy the same rank as the Church. Only redeemed humanity — believers in Jesus Christ — are qualified by creation in the image and likeness of God to make up the corporate Bride and share the Bridegroom's throne.

## The High Position of the Church — God's Original Purpose

It is an awesome thought, but nevertheless true, that God cannot raise up Christian believers any higher in His divine plan without offending the Holy Trinity. While we recognize an immeasurable gulf between the Creator and His creation, it was God's plan from the beginning to bridge this gap. He did this so completely through His Son Jesus Christ that redeemed human beings became full-blooded, genetic members of God's family, seated with Christ on the throne of the universe as His Bride and Companion. "To him who overcomes, I will give the right to sit with me on my throne" (Rev. 3:21, NIV). This was no afterthought. It was God's plan from all eternity. "He chose us in Him before the foundation of the world" (Eph. 1:4, NKJV). *This was God's original purpose in the creation of the universe and the human race. God's unique program of prayer is His method of preparing the Church for her royal position.*

# If the Church Will Not Pray, God Will Not Act

This is why God never goes over the head of His Church to carry out His decisions. He will not take things out of her hands. To do so would undermine His training program. Only by carrying this huge weight of responsibility of prayer can the Church grow into full maturity as co-ruler of the universe. This is why when the Church fails God waits. This is why He will do nothing in the areas of human rescue and restoration until she accepts her part and uses her privilege of intercession. If the Church will not pray, God will not act. Why? He cannot, because if He acted without her, He would stop the process — and therefore His purpose — of bringing His Church to her full potential as His co-ruler.

This was God's plan from the beginning. He will not spoil it now by taking things out of her hands. *He will let the whole world be destroyed first.* His part of the work of redemption is full and complete. He will not override His Church. *His eternal purpose is the qualifying of this Eternal Companion for entering into full partnership with her Lord in the ruling of the universe.* She can only be made ready through the practice of prayer and intercession. Only in this way can she learn to take part in the eternal purpose and plan of her Lord. It follows, then, that *God will do nothing without His Church.*

# Prayer — the Main Business of the Church

This is why the famous 18th century preacher John Wesley said, "God will do nothing but in answer to prayer." This is why S.D. Gordon, 20th century devotional writer, said, "The greatest thing anyone can do for God and for man is to pray." This also explains his statement, "Prayer is striking the winning blow . . . service is gathering up the results." It further clarifies the words of Methodist minister E. M. Bounds (19th century) about prayer: "God shapes the world by prayer. The more praying there is in the world the better the world will be, the mightier the forces against evil . . . the prayers of God's saints are the capital stock of heaven. God conditions the very life and prosperity of His cause on prayer." If these things are true, then prayer should be the main business of our day.

# The Church Holds the Key

The Church actually holds the key. What do we mean by that? Let me illustrate. Checks used by some businesses need the signature of two people to make them good. One signature is not enough. Both people must sign. This helps us understand God's method of operating through the prayers and faith of His people. His promises are His checks signed in His own blood. His part was finished on the cross just outside Jerusalem. Yet, no promise is made good until a redeemed man — a believer in Christ — enters God's throne room and, by prayer and faith, writes his name beside God's. Then, and not until then, are the funds backing the check released. It is like a safe deposit box in a bank vault. The vault keeper has a key and you have a key. Neither key alone will open the box. But, when you give the keeper your key, she inserts *both* keys and the door flies open, making all the treasures in the box available.

*Heaven holds the key by which decisions governing earthly affairs are made, but we hold the key by which those decisions are carried out.* If this is true, then prayer takes on a much greater dimension and importance than people commonly believe. *Prayer is not overcoming resistance in God.* It is not persuading Him to do something He doesn't want to do. No, *prayer is carrying out His decision. It is making His will happen on earth.* Look at Matthew 16:19, NLT, "And I will give you the keys of the Kingdom of Heaven. Whatever you forbid on earth will be forbidden in heaven, and whatever you permit on earth will be permitted in heaven."

Prayer makes it possible for God to do what He wants to do. He cannot operate without it. Remember, all true prayer begins in the heart of God. So, He actually inspires our heart with the prayer and then goes about preparing the answer to that God-inspired prayer before we even speak it. When we truly understand this, then believing for answers becomes easy—far easier than if we had no understanding of God's part in the process.

## Too Busy to Pray

No angel in heaven was ever invited to share this amazing

privilege of prayer. No archangel was ever invited into God's throne room to intercede for the universe. Only true Christians — followers and lovers of Christ. Yet many of us are too busy — watching television, going to movies, following sports, enjoying recreation, pursuing careers, etc., etc. We are so busy with the cares and pleasures of this life — trying to keep up with the latest trend in new cars, new homes, new furniture, new technology, etc., we have no time to pray.

Someone has described a contemporary American as a person who drives a bank-financed car over a bond-financed highway on credit card gas to open a charge account at a department store so he can fill his mortgage company financed home with installment-purchased furniture. Doesn't this description also fit today's Christian? Is it any wonder we have so little time to pray?

You might be thinking: Can't we have anything for ourselves? The answer is NO. Christ should be everything to you. 1 Corinthians 6:19-20 tells us we don't belong to ourselves. We have been bought with a price. And 1 Corinthians 10:31 says, "So whether you eat or drink, or whatever you do, do it all for the glory of God" (NLT). If you can buy the new car, the new home, the new furniture, the newest technological wonder, hold down two jobs, etc., for the glory of God — good for you! Yet, doesn't it stand to reason that if we didn't need all these things we would have much more time to pray? If we were not so hungry for pleasure, travel, vacations, recreation, and more things, wouldn't we have more time to pray? Wouldn't we have more time to pray if we weren't so caught up with sports, movies and entertainment?

Today, we have more free time than ever before — but less time to pray. We are cheating God and the world for whom we should be praying. Yet, we are cheating ourselves. By our failure to pray we are putting an obstacle in God's way — we are preventing Him from accomplishing His heart's desire for the human race. We are robbing the world of God's highest and best plan for it. Thus, we are limiting our own eternal reward and rank in heaven.

## "I SEARCHED FOR SOMEONE TO STAND IN THE GAP...BUT I FOUND NO ONE."

# NOTES

1. Two similar but distinct Greek words are used in this passage: *petros*, a masculine noun translated "Peter," and *petra*, a feminine noun translated "rock." According to *Thayer's Greek Lexicon, petra* means "a massive, living [unquarried] rock" — like Gibraltar — while *petros* signifies "a detached but large fragment." Here Jesus is saying He will build His Church, not on the smaller, detached stone Peter (*petros*), but on the huge rock (*petra),* which of course is Jesus Christ Himself. The statement follows that the gates of hell will not prevail against it.

   In the Orient at that time, the gate of the city was the place of government where court was held and where decisions were made. This is the place where counsel was taken and where strategy and plans for action were shaped. So, Jesus is saying that all of the plans of attack that hell could come up with or invent against His Church would fail.

   To a casual onlooker, this might sound like a useless hope because it seems like Satan is actually winning against God's kingdom. If the contest between God and Satan were for the devotion of the majority of human beings, then clearly Satan is the winner, but if God's real purpose is calling out a specific group of people called the Church, who are being groomed for rulership in His universal kingdom — then, as long as Christ is successfully gathering and preparing His Church, the gates of hell are not taking control. If Satan could somehow prevent the calling out of the Church, then the gates of hell would be victorious. Yet, from the birth of the Church to this present throbbing moment, Satan has never been able to stop Christ's calling out His loved ones to Himself and His service. Through opposition, persecution and even martyrdom the Church has marched on. Neither suffering nor trials or tragedy, neither stress nor persecution or hunger, neither poverty nor danger or weapons of destruction have been able to stop the forward march of the Church. Therefore, the gates of hell have *not* prevailed against the Church.

# NOTES

2.  The mystery of God's heavenly marriage program is intensified by the idea of a multiple bride. To many people this doesn't seem proper because in earthly marriage we think of a bride as a single person. This problem disappears when we understand Paul's concept of the Church as a whole, living body. "The human body has many parts, but the many parts make up one whole body. So it is with the body of Christ....Yes, the body has many different parts, not just one part" (1 Cor. 12:12,14, NLT).

    We consider the human body as a single entity because it is united by a single consciousness. Paul points out that it is not one, but many members. In the same way, the Holy City in John's vision (Rev. 21), which is the heavenly Bride, is inhabited not by one person but by a great multitude of people. Still, because it will be united by a single awareness, it will make up a single, harmonious whole much like we see in the unity of the human body. The Church is moving toward this kind of unity, and it will be fulfilled in absolute perfection by the members of Christ's Bride who will take up residence in the New Jerusalem, which John saw coming down out of heaven from God. That city will be made up of the countless members of the Church who are united by their holy passion for their Bridegroom Jesus Christ. Can this be why God counts unity among His people so important? Could this also be why Satan fights this unity so desperately?

# 4

# Christ's Gift of Authority

*"I have given you authority to trample on snakes and scorpions and to overcome all the power of the enemy; nothing will harm you."* (Luke 10:19, NIV)

## The Church's Magna Carta

When the seventy disciples returned from ministering to the people, they brought the amazing report that even the demons submitted to them. Jesus responded with a startling statement — the importance of which has been missed by many believers. He announced that He had personally watched Satan's removal from heaven. In fact, it was His word of authority that drove Satan out so that he fell from heaven "as lightning" (Luke 10:18). Now, to their further amazement, Jesus actually places in their hands that same word of authority. Now He is saying, "I hand this authority over to you." "I have given you authority to trample on snakes [evil spirits] and scorpions [demons] and to overcome all the power of the enemy [Satan]; nothing will harm you" (Luke 10:19, Heb. 2:14-15).

This is the Church's Magna Carta (document declaring legal rights of free men in 13th century England) in her conflict with Satan. Here is a clear legal basis for freedom from Satan's control and abuse, and for aggressive action against him. *It is clear from this and other Scriptures that God intends the true Church, not Satan, to be in control of human events and happenings.*

# Organic (Living) Unity

In Ephesians 1:20-22, Paul explains that Christ is the highest authority in the universe. His name is far above every other name, power or ruler in all of creation. Paul tells us that everything in heaven and on earth has been put under Christ's feet, that is, under His absolute control. Then Paul adds that Christ is the Head of the Church, which is His body. What does this mean? This is not only a practical relationship but an organic or living relationship as well. This is not a mystical, philosophical, symbolic or organizational relationship; it is living unity.

Let me illustrate. The members of a board of directors of a corporation only have a functional or practical relationship to one another. In contrast, an arm, hand or foot has an organic relationship to the body because each part receives its life from the life of the body. In the same way, Christians have a living relationship to Christ because He is their source of life. The Church isn't some institution or company run by Christ as President or a kingdom over which He is the supreme ruler. No, the Church is an organism, a living thing, vitally connected to Christ, the source of her life.

# Organic Unity Predicted

God paints a picture of this unique kind of living relationship in the story of Adam and Eve. Even after the Lord had created a multitude of life forms to inhabit planet earth, and Adam himself had named them all, no suitable partner for Adam could be found among them. It seems none of these creatures had the same human nature as he. So, God sent Adam into a deep sleep; from a wound in his side God took out a piece of Adams's own body and fashioned the perfect companion for him. "Now there was a being in life who could understand Adam, one who could enter into his plans, ideals, aims, hopes and fears, one who could love as he loved and live as he lived in a manner such as none of the lower orders could" (T.H. Nelson). "At last!" The man exclaimed. "This one is bone from my bone, and flesh from my flesh! She will be called 'woman,' because she was taken from 'man'" (Gen. 2:23, NLT). This was *organic* relationship.

In 1 Corinthians 15:44-47, Christ is called the "second man," the "last Adam." Since Adam symbolized Christ, it stands to reason that Christ must also have a bride. Like the first Adam, He too went into a deep sleep of death and resurrection. Out of Christ's wounded side the Church, through faith, is born of God as the Bride of Christ. In Revelation 21:9 the Church is called the Bride, the Lamb's Wife. In Ephesians 5, the chapter dealing with both earthly and heavenly marriage, Paul tells us in verse 30 that as Eve was part of Adam so we, the Church, are members of His body — His flesh and His bones. The Church is His Body now. She will be His Bride at the Marriage Supper of the Lamb.

## On the Throne Because of This Living Unity

All that we have just discussed supports the concept of this living unity or oneness between Christ and His Church. Think about it. Christ has been lifted up as the Highest Authority in the universe and is now sitting on the right hand of His Father exercising all of the authority of the Trinity, both in heaven and on earth. If the Church as His Body is wholly united with Him as the Head, *where does that place the Church?* Is she not with Christ on His throne? Yes, she is! Paul confirms this with his statement in Ephesians 2:5-6 that after making us alive with Christ, God raised us up together with Him and seated us together in heavenly places. In other words, we have already been *legally* seated on the throne with Christ because we are already one with Him. We are now already ruling and reigning with Him. We are co-crucified, co-raised, co-exalted, and co-seated with Christ.[1]

## Practical Results of Living Unity

To the natural mind this all seems like utter nonsense, but it is true. In spite of all her weaknesses, failures and inexcusable sins, the Church is the greatest force for civilization and educated social consciousness in the world today. It is true in the ancient world that as the knowledge of God and respect for God disappeared moral decay and crimes against others completely destroyed the social order. "Now God saw that the earth had become corrupt and was filled with violence. God observed all this corruption in the world, for everyone on earth was corrupt. So God said to Noah, 'I have decided to destroy all living creatures, for they have filled the earth with violence. Yes, I will wipe them all out along with the earth!'" (Gen. 6:11-13, NLT).

It is the same today. The only force in the world that is

fighting against Satan's total control in human affairs is the Church of the living God. The prayers and holy lives of God's people restrain Satan. If nothing hindered Satan, he would establish hell in this world here and now. The only healing stream in the howling deserts of human life flows from our Savior's cross on Mt. Calvary. The only pure unselfishness in the world comes from the "fountain filled with blood." If not for Christ's completely selfless love displayed for all to see on the bloody cross, total selfishness would rule the world. Total selfishness means total hostility. Total hostility means total anarchy or mob rule, *and that means hell.*

## Civilization Is a By-Product of the Gospel

No stable social order or civilization as we know it can exist without the blessings of peace and tranquility, which are the result of the Gospel. The true Church is the caretaker of that Gospel. Therefore, the true Church is the most central, basic and essential foundation upon which every other structure — social, political, and governmental — depends. The Church is absolutely necessary. Without the moral and spiritual guidance of the Word of God, which the Church communicates to the world, no agreeable environment for business and commerce would exist. Without the Word of God no enlightening cultural, educational or social activities would exist.

Without the knowledge of God and reverence for Him, no orderly and efficient working of government can exist. All of the processes of democracy and civilization, as we know them, need an umbrella of law and order under which to operate. This umbrella or protective covering is kept in place only where the Gospel has spread its gracious and life-giving influence. What we know as Western civilization — providing the highest standard of living, the greatest freedom and personal security, the most homeland peace and calm the world has ever known — is definitely a by-product of the Judeo-Christian moral standards and the redeeming, restoring power of Jesus Christ.

# The Church Controls the Balance of Power

The Gospel is the source of all that is good in the world — all the values, standards and qualities of good character, which are the very basis of our moral, spiritual, social, and political health and well-being. The Church is the guardian and representative of that Gospel. History reveals that, to the same degree the Church has been faithful in her responsibility to the Gospel, she has been the saving and protecting power in human events as well as the major channel of grace and mercy in the world. To the same extent the Church has been faithful, she has controlled the balance of power overcoming the total breakdown and collapse of the world system.

What did Jesus have to say about all this? He was not speaking words of fantasy when He said to His disciples, "You are the salt of the earth . . . You are the light of the world" (Matt. 5:13-14, NKJV). The outside world is totally blind to this fact; if it were not for the cleansing, preserving influence of the Church, the entire structure of all we call civilization would completely fall apart, decay and disappear. At this present pulsating moment, the Church, in partnership with her resurrected, all-powerful Lord, is helping hold the world together. *Because of her vital relationship with Christ, the Ruler of the Universe, the Church — not Satan — holds the balance of power in human affairs.* In reality, the fate of the world is in the hands of nameless saints. This truth is plainly laid out in Psalm 149:5-9, "Let the saints rejoice in this honor and sing for joy on their beds. May the praise of God be in their mouths and a double-edged sword in their hands, to inflict vengeance on the nations and punishment on the peoples, to bind their kings with fetters, their nobles with shackles of iron, to carry out the sentence written against them. This is the glory of all his saints. Praise the Lord" (NIV).

If not for the Church, Satan would have already turned this earth into hell. The fact that the earth has not experienced total devastation, in spite of Satan, proves at least a small part of the Church is operating effectively and is already acting out her queenly role in partnership with her Lord. Even now, through prayer and faith, the Church is being prepared by on-the-job training for her position as co-ruler with Christ over the whole universe, following Satan's final destruction.

## The Church's Authority and Free Will[2]

In general, the truth of these principles in world affairs is fairly well documented. Yet, do these same principles apply in personal and individual cases? For example, in the case of the salvation of a specific person, who holds the balance of power, Satan or the Church? What about free will? Does the God-given authority of the Church reach into the area of free moral agency,[3] that is, man's responsibility for his free choices? Is the Church's given authority agreeable with free will? God says in His Word that it is His will for all men to be saved (1 Tim. 2:4). Since we know that it is God's will to save any person who has not crossed that mysterious point of no return (final hardness of heart: Matt. 12:31-32, Mark 3:28-29), may the Church go ahead and pray for the salvation of a specific person with the assurance that he or she will be saved, or does the Church have to consider the fact that the person is a free moral agent and God never saves any person against his will? *Do we have to say*, as we so often do, that because "so and so" is a free moral agent, all we can do is to pray and leave the rest to God and the individual?

Since God has assured us that it is His will that all people be saved, we can be sure when we pray for someone's salvation we are praying according to His will. Notice what the apostle John says, "And we are confident that he hears us whenever we ask for anything that pleases him. And since we know he hears us when we make our requests, we also know that he will give us what we ask for" (1 John 5:14-15, NLT). Now the question is: Does this promise not count because every person has a free will? Do we have to stand back and watch Satan kidnap a person because God does not rescue anyone against his will? Is it right to say that all we can do is pray and leave the rest to God and the individual?

## Weren't We All Rebels?

I'll answer that question by asking another. *Do you believe anyone was ever saved who was not, in the beginning, a rebel?* Weren't all of us born with our backs against God? Didn't we all, just like Adam, run and hide from God? Haven't we all resisted the tugging of God's Spirit on our hearts? Didn't we all keep on resisting that inner tug until it became so overwhelming it was easier to say yes to God than to continue rebelling against Him? Didn't we all come to a point where somehow our rebellion turned into surrender, not because our wills were forced, but because it was more painful to resist than to give in? Though we did surrender, we could have chosen to continue operating our lives in defiance.

## What Is the Deciding Factor in Salvation?

Isn't this the general pattern of the journey from rebellion to surrender? Jesus says, "No one can come to me unless the Father who sent me draws him" (John 6:44, NIV). The Father always pulls us toward Him by the power of His Spirit. Let's think about this. Since God loves everyone, wants everyone to be saved and faithfully looks for all of us, *why* is the Holy Spirit able to persuade some but not others? Could it be that in some situations God is so powerless He can't convince the person to be saved, or is it possible some people are the targets of powerful, believing prayer while others don't have anyone praying for them? If 18th century preacher John Wesley is correct in saying "God does nothing but in answer to prayer," then this must include the salvation of souls. *Thus, no person is saved without someone praying for him; every person who commits his life to Christ does so because of the prayers of someone who would not give him up to Satan.*

We agree that God wants to save everyone. He has provided salvation for all. John the Baptist announced, "Look, the Lamb of God who takes away the sin of the world" (John 1:29, NIV). "He himself is the sacrifice that atones [pays for] our sins — and not only our sins but the sins of *all the world*"

(1 John 2:2, NLT). However, though God's will for all to be saved was proven by the provision of that salvation through Christ, *this salvation is limited entirely by the intercession, or lack of it, by the Church. Those for whom the Church prays are saved. All others are lost.* Yes, the work of the Church in prayer is the deciding factor in a person's salvation. "And with that he breathed on them and said, 'Receive the Holy Spirit. If you forgive anyone his sins, they are forgiven; if you do not forgive them, they are not forgiven'" (John 20:22-23, NIV)[4]

## The Spirit and the Bride

The Holy Spirit has the ability to enlighten our minds, to wake up our spirits and to move our emotions in such a way that we will find it easier to give in to Him rather than refuse Him. *Yet, God will not go over the head of His Church even to save a soul. He must have her cooperation. If she will not intercede, the Holy Spirit, by His own choice, cannot do His assigned work of showing us our sins and convincing us of our need of a Savior.* Because God's purpose is to prepare His Bride for eternal rulership with Him, He has chosen to save no person until His Church cries out for that person's salvation. "The Spirit *and* the Bride say, 'Come!'" (Rev. 22:17) — not the Spirit alone, but the Spirit *and* the Bride. *He will do nothing without her.* Therefore, He *can* do nothing without her.[5]

If the Church does not struggle in prayer for lost souls, the Spirit does not pursue them. If the Spirit does not pursue and draw people to God, then they will be lost. Yet, the Spirit can and will pursue; *when* the Church does the work of prayer He can and will persuade any person, who has not hardened his heart, to come to Christ.

## The Power of Life or Death

If these things are true, the Church — not Satan — holds the balance of power in world events and the salvation of individual human beings. *Thus, a holy Church, by her prayers or lack of them, holds the power of life or death over the souls of men.* Without forcing a person's free will, the Spirit can so powerfully persuade him that he will freely choose to surrender. Yet, the Spirit does this only in answer to the faith and prayer of the Church. Could this be why some people are strongly convicted and converted to Christ while others are not?

## The Damascus Road Experience

It's helpful to look at the conversion of the apostle Paul in regard to this point of the balance of power. We aren't told specifically that the Church was praying for Saul, its most feared enemy, but can anyone doubt that they were? When the apostle Peter was in prison, Acts 12:5 tells us "constant prayer was offered to God for him by the church" (NKJV). We can hardly doubt that sincere prayers were prayed for Saul since the very safety and life of the Church was at stake. It is easy to believe that much intercession was made for his salvation; this prayer even made it possible for him to be confronted by the risen Christ on the Damascus Road — a confrontation that changed him from the Church's worst enemy into its greatest apostle. The apostle's free will was not forced. He was simply convinced that submitting his will to Christ was the best choice. If the prayers of the Church could bring about such a dramatic conversion, is *anyone* beyond the reach of God's Spirit when the Church joins with the Spirit through the work of prayer?

## Paul's Mighty Weapons

You might not be convinced that these principles regarding prayer have such power over a person's free will and personal responsibility. Simply because of the free will of human beings, you may doubt the Church has authority in personal and individual cases. Maybe you still feel that, concerning the salvation of a specific person, all we can do is pray and leave the rest to God and that individual. Let's take a look at Paul's comments in 2 Corinthians 10:4-5: "I use God's mighty weapons, not those made by man, to knock down the devil's strongholds. These weapons can break down every proud argument against God and every wall that can be built to keep men from finding him. *With these weapons I can capture rebels and bring them back to God, and change them into men whose hearts' desire is obedience to Christ*" (TLB).[6]

## Freedom of Choice

Do you think Paul was ignoring the free will and moral responsibility of people when he wrote these words, or was he thinking of the way the Holy Spirit knocked him off his horse that day on the Damascus Road even while he was breathing out violence against Christ and His followers? Was he remembering the sound of that heavenly voice? Was he perhaps thinking about how his own heart melted and was instantly changed by the powerful work of the Holy Spirit so that he desired to obey Christ? Was his faith inspired because he realized these same weapons, which changed him from a rebel into a willing "captive" of Christ, could be just as powerful in his hands to capture rebels and bring them back to God?

Notice that in the use of these weapons Paul does not go against the freedom of choice of the rebels. He does not use force. No, he uses these weapons to change men from rebels to the voluntarily redeemed. Their free will is not violated. They become willing "captives" of Christ. Let me ask this: If such weapons were available to Paul, aren't they also available to the Church, to whom Christ has given authority over all the power of the enemy?

## A Rebel Won to Christ

My mother used these same weapons on me. I was as hostile to God as any sinner. I was fighting with all my might. Yet, the time came when it was easier to lay down my weapons than to continue my fight. The constant pressure of the Holy Spirit on me became so powerful that I finally looked for relief by giving up my rebellious will. I felt God's love so strongly that I freely chose to fall into His arms of grace. I became a willing "captive."

God can and does work with any sinner in this same way when the Church learns to use these mighty weapons of persistent, determined prayer and faith. It is my firm belief that wherever a person has not crossed the deadline of final hardness of heart, a believing Church may pray with total assurance and faith for that person's salvation.

**"YET NO SOONER IS ZION [THE CHURCH] IN LABOR THAN SHE GIVES BIRTH TO HER CHILDREN"** (Isa. 66:8, NIV)

# NOTES

1. To many people this is an impossible mystery, a riddle that cannot be understood, a puzzle that cannot be solved. How can we be united with Christ and be seated with Him in heaven when we are living life as usual with our feet resting on solid ground? Paul offers a key to this mystery in 1 Corinthians 6:17: "But the person who is joined to the Lord is one spirit with him" (NLT). In some philosophical systems, spirit is considered to be essential reality. Material (physical things) is said to be accidental; that is, it takes its reality from its relationship to spirit. For instance, when the spirit leaves the body, the body breaks down and decays. It loses its form because it depends on the spirit for its organization as reality. The spirit has independent reality; it exists on its own. The body has only relative or conditional existence. It is the spirit that gives life to the body and keeps it going. This is what we mean when we say the spirit is essential reality and material is only accidental, or has only relative reality. In other words, your spirit is the real you, the real person. Therefore, it makes sense that a person who is joined to the Lord as one spirit is, in his essential being, seated beside Christ in the heavens. While the body is here, the real self is there. While a body may only be in one place at a time, the spirit is not so limited. Because it is true that he that is joined to the Lord is one spirit, it is also true, since Christ is exalted and seated on His throne, the Church is exalted and seated on His throne with Him.

2. Nothing in this or the following paragraphs should imply that the sinner is released in any way from full responsibility for his own salvation. The Church's responsibility ends with her faithful prayers. Only the Holy Spirit knows when that point is reached. The sinner is totally responsible. The Church's responsibility is restricted by the principle of free moral agency — a person is responsible for his own free will choices.

3. The term "free moral agency" is not used here in its complete sense, since God alone is absolutely "free." However, even though man's will has been warped by the fall (Adam and

# NOTES

Eve's sin of disobedience in the Garden of Eden), he is still responsible for his decisions.

4.  The meaning of John 20:23 has often been up for discussion: "If you forgive anyone his sins, they are forgiven; if you do not forgive them, they are not forgiven" (NIV). It almost shocks us that Christ has given authority for the forgiveness of sins to the disciples and therefore to the Church. Yet, in a very real sense this is true. By using her God-given authority of prayer and faith, the Church opens the way for the Holy Spirit to do His work of conviction and persuasion. Through the work of the Spirit, in answer to the believing prayer of the true Church, the sinner is brought to the place of turning away from sin by his own free will and is given faith to receive forgiveness. God, the only One who has power to forgive sin, offers the actual pardon and forgiveness. However, because all this takes place as a result of the Church's earnest prayers, she is truly involved in this absolution (pardon). This is why Jesus could say to the disciples and to a holy Church, "If you forgive anyone his sins, they are forgiven; if you do not forgive them, they are not forgiven" (John 20:23, NIV). In a very real sense, then, the responsibility for pardon is in the hands of a praying Church.

5.  In the Old Testament, the nation of Israel was considered to be the wife of Jehovah. Since the Church, in a spiritual sense, is the "new Israel," it seems fair to think of the Church as having inherited this same wifely relationship, though the Marriage Supper of the Lamb has not yet been celebrated. "Therefore, my brethren, you also have become dead to the law through the body of Christ, that you may be married to another — to Him who was raised from the dead, that we should bear fruit to God" (Rom. 7:4, NKJV). Think about the birth of a new baby. It's a process that involves the consent and cooperation of both the father and the mother. That new life does not enter the world without some degree of pain and struggle. Think about this as an analogy reflecting the work of the Spirit of God and the Church who must agree and cooperate in bringing newborn

# NOTES

souls into the family of God. This spiritual process also involves struggle and work. *Soul-winning is not easy.* It is necessary for the Spirit and the Church to work together. By His own choice, the Spirit alone cannot bring a soul to birth. The Church's part as intercessor is just as important as the Spirit's part. The Spirit and the Bride say, "Come!"

6. It is recognized that the accuracy of the paraphrase is applicable to the point at issue.

# 5
# The Legal Basis of the Authority of the Church

## Was Calvary a Victory or a Defeat?

**W**e must ask this question because it is absolutely necessary for every believer to know with certainty that Christ's death on Calvary was an inexpressibly brilliant triumph and victory. Christians must completely understand and be totally convinced of this sure basis of their faith, or they will be bothered by doubts and will not be able to confidently take authority over Satan. Chapters 5 and 6 are designed to take away any such doubt and to show that Christ, through the cross at Calvary and His descent into hell itself, totally and without any doubt defeated and stripped Satan of power — both legally and in his operations. The apostle Paul refers to the satanic forces as "the dethroned powers that rule" (1 Cor. 2:6, *Moffatt*).

It is interesting that the reality of Christ's victory at Calvary has been openly challenged by the church of Satan, an organization still alive and well in our society. They represent Calvary as a defeat, a stupid display of feeble weakness.

According to *The Satanic Bible*, the crucifix symbolizes "pallid incompetence hanging on a tree." In *The Satanic Rituals* Satan is called "the ineffable Prince of Darkness who rules the earth." He is pictured as taking the initiative from

Christ, who is called "the lasting foulness of Bethlehem," "the cursed Nazarene," "impotent king," "fugitive and mute god," "vile and abhorred pretender to the majesty of Satan."

Satan is described as "great Satan," "Prince of Darkness," "Satan — Lucifer who rules the earth," who will send the "Christian minions staggering to their doom." He is painted as "the Lord of Light" — with Christ's angels, cherubim and seraphim "cowering and trembling with fear" and "prostrating themselves before him" while he "sends the gates of heaven crashing down."

This is just one example of the way Satan constantly tries to persuade the Church and the world that he is almost, if not quite, as powerful as God. The world seems to be pretty well convinced by this deception, and the Church suffers a kind of anxiety because of its pressure. Satan has successfully hidden from the Church what actually happened to him, not only at Calvary, but also between Calvary and the resurrection of Christ. Why does Calvary appear to be a defeat to some believers and the world at large? It seems in spite of our declared faith in Christ, many of us are hounded with the sneaking suspicion that Satan was, after all, the winner here. Yet, a careful look into the legal phases of the great battle between Christ and Satan proves once and for all that Christ was the true champion and conqueror. The legal perspective of His victory is the theme of this chapter.

## Adam's Mandate:
## Take Charge of the Earth

In order to grasp what actually happened at Calvary, we

must understand what took place legally in the fall in the Garden of Eden. Man was originally made for authority. He was created for ruling. When he came from God's hand he was given the rulership of planet earth, the kingship of its life and the control and mastery over its rich resources. Genesis 1:26 tells us, "Then God said, 'Let us make man in our image, in our likeness, and let them rule over the fish of the sea and the birds of the air, over the livestock, over all the earth, and over all the creatures that move along the ground" (NIV). The writer of the eighth Psalm adds this comment: "You made him ruler over the works of your hands; you put everything under his feet."

## Adam's Tragic Failure

Law governs the whole universe. The plan of God's redemption (restoring fallen man) from beginning to end is based on a system of divine jurisprudence (body or system of laws, legal rules). God's plan has a legal basis. His grant of authority and rulership over the earth to man was a *bona fide* or genuine gift. This authority and dominion became *legally* his. What man did with it was his responsibility. If, so to speak, he fumbled the ball and lost it — which he did when he disobeyed God's instructions — God could not lawfully step in and take it back for him.

Our all-powerful God undoubtedly had the power to cancel Satan's victory over Adam, Eve and their inheritance from God, but this would have gone against His own moral principles of government. If God had gone over man's head and reclaimed the title to the earth from Satan by force, He would have done it without due process of law.

## God's Search for a "Legal" Challenger

When Adam chose to obey Satan rather than God, he became Satan's slave. "Don't you know that when you offer yourselves to someone to obey him as slaves, you are slaves to the one whom you obey — whether you are slaves to sin, which leads to death, or to obedience, which leads to righteousness?" (Rom. 6:16, NIV). As a slave of Satan, Adam lost all of his legal rights — not only his personal rights, but also the rights to his God-given territory, which was the earth. This gave Satan legal authority to rule over both man and the earth. If Satan's rulership was to be cancelled, a way had to be found to redeem fallen man and restore his lost authority without going against the universal rules of justice.

Since Satan was now the rightful owner of Adam and the legal ruler of the earth, God had no moral right, under His own code of justice, to simply put an end to it. No angel could get into the contest because these legal rights were never extended to the angels. Instead, a member of Adam's race had to be found who could qualify to file a lawsuit against Satan in the universal court and legally reclaim from him Adam's lost inheritance and rulership. The government of the earth had been given to man. Man lost it. Only a man could legally take it back.

Where was the man who could do this? Since Adam was Satan's slave, all of his children and descendants, would be Satan's slaves also. A slave has no legal standing and cannot go to court or lawfully take part in a legal process. It follows that no son of Adam could qualify to even enter the contest. A member of the human race had to be found on whom Satan had no claim; the human redeemer had to be a challenger who could qualify to bring against Satan a lawsuit, which would cancel his legal right to rule over humanity and planet earth.

## Problem Solved: The Incarnation

To the human mind the situation was hopeless, but *God found a way.* "But when the time had fully come, God sent his son, born of a woman, born under the law, to redeem those under law, that we might receive the full rights of sons" (Gal. 4:4-5, NIV). *God solved the problem by the Incarnation* (Jesus becoming human). Because the Holy Spirit gave Jesus human life, He was NOT the fallen son of Adam. Therefore, Satan had no claim on Him. Yet, because He was born of a woman, He was a real human being and could qualify as a true member of the human race. He could take on the legal fight against Satan and reclaim all that Adam had lost.

## Why Was the Virgin Birth Necessary?

Some people say it does not make any difference whether Jesus was divine or not. They say nothing can ever change the life He lived, the truth He taught, or His contribution to the world; this is terribly faulty logic. If Jesus were the son of Joseph and Mary, or the son of Mary and someone else (as some critics have blasphemously suggested), He would have been Adam's descendant, as well as Satan's slave, just like everyone else. He would have been disqualified to challenge Satan in court. This would not work. To be legally recognized as plaintiff (accuser or prosecutor), a man had to be found who was truly human but not a descendant of

Adam. Therefore, *the Virgin Birth was absolutely necessary.* "The angel replied, 'The Holy Spirit will come upon you, and the power of the Most High will overshadow you. So the baby to be born will be holy, and he will be called the Son of God'" (Luke 1:35, NLT).

## Why a Perfect Man?

The Virgin Birth was necessary for another reason as well. Satan's Challenger had to be a true human being who, under testing, would prove to be a perfect, sinless man. Satan could have no claim on him. So, this Champion of the human race had to live an absolutely pure and sinless life. If Jesus were not the Son of God by Mary, *who became pregnant and gave birth to Him supernaturally,* then He was simply the son of Adam. If He were the son of Adam, He would have inherited Adam's sin. If He had inherited Adam's sin, He could not have lived a sinless life. If He had not lived a sinless life, He would have come under Satan's control and would have been morally disqualified to take on the legal conflict against Satan. *In order to meet the legal standard, Christ had to be truly human. In order to meet the moral standard of perfection, He had to be divine, the actual Son of God.*

## Jesus Confronts Satan as a Man

Jesus came to earth as a real human being. Because He was conceived by the Holy Spirit and born of a virgin, Satan had no legal claim on Him. Satan had to contrive a legal basis to take authority over Him. He had to try to tempt Jesus in such a way he would ruin the Lord's perfect track record and cause Him to sin in some way. Satan could succeed only if he could break up the close relationship Jesus had with His Father; he had to pressure Him to rebel and do things on His own. This was Satan's master plan. *This was the whole basis of the struggle between Jesus and the archfiend of darkness.* Why was it so important? The destiny of the entire world and the human race rested on the outcome of this great struggle. If Satan could, by any means possible, force Jesus to have just one thought out of harmony with His Heavenly Father, he would be the winner and stay in control of the earth and the human race. If he could fool the Last Adam (Jesus) as he did the first Adam, his rulership over the world and mankind would be forever certain.

Although Jesus was "very God of very God" (Nicene Creed), He had to fight this battle and overcome as a true man. In this struggle, it would have been against universal justice and would have been an empty victory for Jesus to use divine weapons and resources, which were not available to the first Adam in the Garden of Eden. Yes, though Jesus had all the resources of Heaven at His fingertips, *solely as a pure, sinless Man, He took on Satan in this critical contest.*

## The Battle of the Ages

From Bethlehem to Calvary, the conflict raged. In His effort to win back the lost inheritance of the first Adam, Jesus and the fallen Lucifer — son of the morning — were locked in mortal combat. Through His 33 years of life, the struggle continued with no reprieve. The fallen Lucifer — once the Light Bearer, the guardian of the throne of God, the highest of all created beings before Adam — called together all the resources of the underworld in order to break down the loyalty and devotion of the God-man to His beloved Heavenly Father. If Satan could expose just one weakness, one thought of rebellion or self-will in Jesus, he could stop Him — the Heavenly Champion — from taking back the world and its enslaved human race. That perverted prince of darkness put great effort into forcing a breakdown of Jesus' obedience to His Father throughout His years in Nazareth, during the Temptation in the wilderness, in the opposition of the scribes and Pharisees to His ministry, in the Garden of Gethsemane, in Pilate's judgment hall, and finally in the crisis of Calvary. Satan's aim was to transfer Jesus' loyalty to himself.

## The Wilderness Temptation

In the desert wilderness, Satan offered Jesus a shortcut to world domination if He would only fall down and worship him just once. Satan claimed authority over all the kingdoms of the world had been given to him and that he could give it to anyone he chose. Jesus did not challenge this claim because He knew Satan's legal basis for it. He also knew the only way He could redeem humanity and recover all that was lost was by way of the cross. He overcame Satan's temptation by using the Word of God, *the same Word that was and is available to Adam and all his descendants.* We know that Adam did not have the written Word in the Garden, but he did have the spoken Word, which he heard every day as he walked with the second Person of the Trinity, the pre-incarnate Christ and Eternal Word.

# The Garden of Gethsemane

The battle, which continued through His years of ministry, reached an unbelievable peak in the Garden of Gethsemane where Jesus prayed before His crucifixion. The demonic pressure on His spirit was so crushing it brought Him to the very brink of death. While drops of blood oozed from His tortured face and splattered on the ground, Jesus cried out, "My soul is overwhelmed with sorrow to the point of death" (Matt. 26:38, NIV). Our minds can't handle this mental picture and we have no words to describe it. As God, Jesus could have commanded thousands of angels to come help Him, but if He had done this He would not have suffered only as a man.

# The Real Pain and Suffering

It was not just the dreadful looking ahead to the physical suffering that brought Jesus pain in the Garden. That was nothing compared to the torture of His spirit. It was that horrible anguish of a pure soul who had never known sin having to face the injustice of being "made sin." "He made Him who knew no sin *to be* sin on our behalf, so that we might become the righteousness of God in Him" (2 Cor. 5:21, NASB). It was necessary for Jesus to so completely identify with sin that He gave up His close relationship with His Father as *He actually became the object of the Father's disgust and scorn.* This was no mere legal imputation or charge of sin. HE WAS MADE SIN. *He became the very reality of sin by dying as a sin offering* (as in the Old Testament).

Jesus suffered the ugliness of sin just as if He had actually committed the complete range of human wrongdoing. He was considered guilty of all the sin of all mankind. He was condemned to pay the full price and completely satisfy the demands of justice against the combined sin of the entire world.

The temptation of Gethsemane was to refuse to drink the "cup." Would He try to keep the fellowship He had with His Father before the world began, or would He accept this unjust, yet genuine identification with sin? It was no simulated temptation. This was for real. This reality was what caused His soul to be overwhelmed with sorrow to the point of death. The Lord's indescribable pain is seen in His bloody sweat and His prayer, "O My Father, if it is possible, let this cup pass from Me; *nevertheless*, not as I will, but as You *will*" (Matt. 26:39, NKJV).

It seems this is the highest point of our Lord's suffering. If ever there was any doubt as to the outcome of that suffering, it faded after this. "Nevertheless" — on that one word hung the fate of the entire world. With that decision the crisis passed. He accepted the "cup." He proved Himself worthy (Rev. 5:12). After this dramatic moment, what followed was almost anticlimactic. The judgment hall with its cruel beating and crown of thorns, the tortuous Via Dolorosa leading to Golgotha, and even the actual crucifixion were like the calm following the storm until that actual moment of forsaking. In that moment — as the demons of hell cried out for His blood and His beloved Heavenly Father hid His face — the heart that could take no more was broken, and He dropped His sacred head and died.

## Satan Was Conquered by Death

Satan had worked feverishly to force Jesus to rebel against His Heavenly Father and transfer His loyalty to himself. He pushed Jesus all the way to death, "even the death of the cross" (Phil. 2:8 KJV). Satan was completely defeated and crushed when Jesus — without one time failing in His obedience to His Heavenly Father — finally bowed His head in deathly agony and gave up His spirit. Satan's purpose was to force Jesus to think just one small thought of rebellion against His Father, but our Lord died without giving way to that pressure. Satan had gone too far. Christ conquered him through His death.

If we take a close look at the results of Christ's death on Calvary, the amazing truth will hit us: His death was THE TRIUMPH OF THE AGES, the greatest victory against evil the world has ever known. Jesus died without failing in even one small detail — He never sinned. This completely defeated Satan's purpose to obtain a claim on Him. Furthermore, His innocent death canceled all of Satan's legal claims of rulership over the earth and the whole human race. Under universal law, when a man commits murder, he is at the mercy of the death penalty. A convicted murderer must give up his life. He actually destroys himself.

When Satan forced the death of Jesus Christ he became, for the first time in his ancient history, a *murderer*.[1] Satan, who had the power of death, had freely killed millions since the fall of Adam because he had a legal right to do so. As a slave-owner, Satan had legal ownership of Adam and all of his descendants. He could do with them whatever he wanted, but he had now made the greatest mistake of his evil career.

In his desperate attempts to break up Jesus' total union with His Father, he killed an innocent Man upon whom he had no actual legal claim. By doing this, he committed murder; in the court of divine justice, he brought to himself the sentence of death. This helps us understand the meaning of Hebrews 2:14: "Since the children have flesh and blood, he too shared in their humanity *so that by his death he might destroy [make powerless] him who holds the power of death — that is, the devil*" (NIV). If this means anything, it means that Satan is now destroyed — not completely taken out, but rendered ineffective. It means that all of his legal claims against the earth and mankind are totally canceled. A person under the final sentence of death has no legal rights at all. *We can firmly say that since Christ died at Calvary, Satan has absolutely no rights and no claims against anyone or anything. Any authority he took with him when he was thrown out of heaven has passed into the hands of the new Man, Jesus Christ, along with all the lost inheritance of Adam. All has been restored by the* **TRIUMPH OF THE CRUCIFIED ONE. HALLELUJAH!**

# NOTES

1. This does not conflict with John 8:44. We read in 1 John 3:15 that "Whoever hates his brother is a murderer" (NKJV). In this sense Satan was a murderer from the beginning, but in a legal sense he became a murderer only when he killed Jesus.

## CHAPTER NUMBER
# 6
# Christ's Dynamic Victory

## Christ's Descent Into Hell

Christ's victory was not only legal; it was dynamic. What does that mean? His victory was powerful; it was won by using unstoppable force. Because He was "made sin" (2 Cor. 5:21), actually became the very essence of sin on the cross, He was removed from God's presence as a disgusting, repulsive thing. He and sin were made the same thing. To become a true substitute for us, He had to satisfy the rights demanded by justice all by Himself as if He were actually guilty of the sum total of the sin of the whole world. His soul was made an offering for sin, the sin of all the generations of the human race (Isa. 53:10). *Eternal justice could not survive if it tried to ignore the sins of the race.* That would make it a farce, pure make-believe.

Justice demanded the full penalty for every sin of all mankind be paid by someone. This meant it was not enough for Christ to give up only His physical life on the cross.[1] His *pure human spirit had to descend into hell* (Eph. 4:9, Acts 2:27). He was a real person with body, soul and spirit. His spirit must not only go down into hell, but down into the lowest hell. *The highest price had to be paid. He must "taste death for every man"* (Heb. 2:9, KJV). *To effectively stand in our place, Christ had to pay the ultimate price — once, for all — for the eternal*

71

*consequences of the combined sin of the whole world.* Thus, He took on Himself everything humanity could possibly suffer.

T. H. Nelson said, "If Christ in spirit did not thus 'descend into hell,' then we have no legal ground of assurance that we may escape that horrid prison." The heavenly Father turned Him over — not only to the agony and death of Calvary, but to the satanic torturers — as part of the fair price for the sins of the human race. As long as Christ was the essence of sin, He was at Satan's mercy in that place of torment where all unrepentant sinners are taken captive when they leave this life (Luke 16:19-31). This seems to be the headquarters from which Satan operates (Rev. 9:1-2, 11).

While Christ was identified with sin, Satan and the demons of hell ruled over Him just as they would rule over any lost sinner. During that seemingly endless period of time He spent in the darkness of death, Satan did with Him what he wanted, and all of hell celebrated. This is part of what Jesus suffered for us.

## The Sufferings of Divine Justice

Some believe the misery Christ experienced in that dark prison is described in Psalm 88: "He [the Father] laid him in the lowest pit, the pit of the underworld, in the dark place, in dense darkness. I [Jesus] am full of trouble, weighted with evils. Thou hast brought me to Sheol, the kingdom of death. I am become a man without God. Thy wrath lieth hard upon me. Thy wrath presseth, thou hast laid thy fury upon me. Thou hast let all thy waves strike me. I have called upon thee, my God, day and night; and thou hearest me not. I have borne thy terrors so that I am distracted — helpless. The outbursts of thy wrath, thy streams of wrath have cut me *off*" (*Cross Reference Bible*, verses 6, 3, 5, 7, 9, 15-16). Our human mind can never understand the extent of pain He went through during the seeming eternity in that demonic pit. Perhaps the prophet Isaiah described it best when he said, "He poured out His soul unto death" (Isa. 53:12, NKJV). He suffered in our place, until — in the mind of God — the conditions of eternal justice were fully met. "He shall see the labor of His soul, and be satisfied" (Isa. 53:11, NKJV).

## The Pain of the Father

We stand amazed at Jesus' willingness to drink that awful cup of pain, but we are in danger of forgetting that God (the Father) so loved the world that He gave His only begotten Son. Jesus was not the only one who suffered in the Trinity. It is very hard to imagine what the Father felt when He had to turn His back on the Son of His love to provide full payment for our sins. *This forsaking by His Father was the essence, the very heart, of Jesus' punishment and suffering; it was the heart of the Father's sorrow as well.* However, for the Father, another terrible cost is expressed in Romans 8:32: "He that spared not his own Son, *but delivered him up for us all,* how shall he not with him also freely give us all things?" Eternal judgment against sin could not be taken care of by simply turning His Son over to the horrible tortures of Satan. No, justice required that the full force of the Father's own displeasure and anger against the combined sin of the human race be poured out on our Lord, with nothing held back. Look again at the Psalm 88 passage already quoted.

*Try to imagine what it must have cost the Father to heap the full force of His anger against all the sins of all mankind on His innocent, perfect and beloved Son.* The Father could not escape this requirement. In fact, Isaiah the prophet spelled it all out centuries before Christ's crucifixion. "But it was the LORD's good plan to crush him and cause him grief. Yet when his life is made an offering for sin, he will have many descendants. He will enjoy a long life, and the LORD's good plan will prosper in his hands. When he [the Father] sees all that is accomplished by his anguish, he [the Father] will be satisfied. And because of his experience, my righteous servant will make it possible for many to be counted righteous, for he will bear all their sins" (Isa. 53:10-11, NLT).

To the Father, this was the cost that could not be counted in order to bring into being a true family of His very own. His family would not be created only, as were the angels, but also generated or born again members of His own household. Further, since Jesus offered Himself through the eternal Spirit (Heb. 9:14), all the members of the Trinity shared together in the price of this amazing plan of redemption.

## Christ's Conflict and Victory in the Depths of Hell

What really happened to Christ in hell? Once the claims of eternal justice were completely carried out, He was justified in the spirit (1 Tim. 3:16, ASV). Then, He was made alive in the spirit (1 Peter 3:18, ASV). His spirit was not totally destroyed. It only died spiritually like any sinful human spirit. It was completely cut off and separated from God. Thus, to be made alive to God and restored to fellowship with His

Father, our Lord had to be reborn. Why? He had become the very essence of sin. Since sin had cut Him off from His Father, the only way He could get back in fellowship with the Father was through a new birth to new life. This is the meaning of Revelation 1:5: "Jesus Christ . . . the first begotten of the dead (KJV).

As long as He was indentified with sin, He was in the clutches of Satan and the demons of hell, just like any lost sinner. Yet, the tables were turned when He was justified, made alive, examined and found innocent and righteous in the Supreme Court of the universe.

The battle in that dark pit of hell is described by Peter in Acts 2:24: "But God released him from the horrors of death and raised him back to life, for *death could not keep him in its grip*" (NLT). This scripture implies hell was in an uproar, scrambling to keep its death hold on Christ. Yet, when He, as a true human being, had completely stripped and humiliated the chief enemy of God and man, He burst out victoriously from that ancient prison of the dead.

Paul says, "Having spoiled principalities and powers [spiritual rulers and authorities], He made a show of them openly, triumphing over them in it" (Col. 2:15, KJV). *According to Webster's New World Dictionary* this word "spoiled" means to "strip the hide from an animal," to "completely disarm a defeated foe," to "damage or injure in such a way as to make useless," to "destroy." This is exactly what Jesus did to Satan after He was justified and made alive in the spirit. The huge struggle that took place in that dark prison is implied in the words, "death could not keep him it its grip."

Death did everything it could to chain Him, to keep Him forever in its power. All of the resources of the underworld were summoned to keep Christ's resurrection from happening, but they all failed. It was impossible for death to keep its prey. In the words of the psalm writer, "he breaks down gates of bronze and cuts through bars of iron" (Psalm 107:16, NIV). From hell's struggle the Lord came out the winner, holding the keys of death and hell. "I am the Living One; I was dead, and behold I am alive for ever and ever! And I hold the keys of death and Hades [hell]" (Rev. 1:18, NIV). Michelangelo gave us his perspective on this event in one of his famous paintings. He shows the doorway of that dark prison house unhinged at Jesus' command, with a demon crushed under the fallen gate. Truly, death could not hold Him.

An eloquent writer has described the resurrection scene and Christ's ascension into the heavenly kingdom like this: "Forcing a mighty earthquake, He mounted up again to solid earth, the light of day, and to the world of breathing men. Up and up again through the rent clouds and ranks of shouting angels and under the lifted heads of the everlasting doors, until He took His seat at the right hand of the Majesty in the heavens. In the realms of space, in the kingdoms of the universe, in the regions of light or darkness, in the epochs of eternity, there are none to rival our Lord Jesus and no power that does not owe Him tribute. In the nether abyss He has no unconquered challenger. In the heavenlies, it seems there are thrones higher and lower and names more or less eminent, but *He* stands clear above them all. The Christ who died on the cross, who rose from the grave in human form, is exalted as a human being to share the Father's glory and dominion, is filled with God's own fullness, and made without limitation or exception Head over *all* things." Yes, today an authentic, real human being sits on the throne of the universe, commanding all the power of the holy Trinity.

## Christ's Seat of Honor and the Church's Place on His Throne

When Christ took His royal seat in the heavens, He proved undoubtedly that Satan's defeat was complete, that he was absolutely finished. Hell was thrown into total bankruptcy. A supremely superior force stripped Satan of his weapons as well as his legal authority and power. Yet, this was not all. When Jesus broke out of that dark prison and ascended to the heights (Eph. 4:8), *all believers were raised up and seated together with Him*. "But God . . . brought us to life with Christ . . . .And in union with Christ Jesus he raised us up and enthroned us with him in the heavenly realms" (Eph. 2:4-6, NEB).

## Christians Are Identified With Christ in His Death and Resurrection

In the mind of God, every believer shares complete identification with Christ from the cross to the throne. According to God's Word, we are crucified with Him, buried with Him, raised with Him, exalted with Him, and seated on His throne with Him (Rom. 6, Eph. 2). How can we possibly understand this? Let's look at the following.

The combined sin of the world could not be laid upon Him by itself, without the sinner himself. There is no such thing as abstract sin — sin with no sinner. Not only was the sinner's sin placed on Christ, but the person of the sinner was also placed upon Him. Therefore, when He went to the cross He carried the entire human race with Him. "For Christ's love compels us, because we are convinced that one died for all, and therefore all died" (2 Cor. 5:14, NIV). "I have been crucified with Christ; and it is no longer I who live, but Christ lives in me" (Gal. 2:20, NASV). "It is a faithful saying: For if we be dead with him, we shall also live with him" (2 Tim. 2:11, KJV). All mankind was identified with Him in death, *but only those who believe are identified with Him in His resurrection and in His place of honor and glory.*

## Christians Are Identified With Christ in His Place of Honor on His Throne

We are not surprised that *He* is raised up and seated on a throne in the heavens. What is hard for us to understand is that *we* have been honored with Him. Yet, if the scripture says, "he who unites himself with the Lord is one with him in spirit" (1 Cor. 6:17, NIV), then it cannot be any other way. We are not surprised that all things have been put under *His* feet. What surprises us is that as part of Him, His Body, all things are also legally under our feet. What we do not seem to realize is that He is the head over all things *to the Church* (Eph. 1:22). This means that *His leadership over everything is accepted and is in force for the benefit and blessing of the Church,* and is used to fulfill His purpose for her.

*We have not understood the extreme importance of the Church in God's master plan. She is the center and reason of all His activity from all eternity.* He doesn't do anything just for His own sake. He is always thinking of her and including her as a cherished partner in all His plans. The Church is His Body — the completeness of Him that fills all things everywhere. *He is not complete without His Church, which is His Body.*

We must keep in mind these things are only true because God chooses to limit Himself. In the absolute sense, God is entirely self-sufficient. He needs nothing and can be served by no one. Yet, He has freely chosen to limit Himself in order to make the Church His official and legal equal. It is true that the Body cannot function without the Head. It is just as true that the Head, by His own choice, cannot operate without the Body. Both are equally necessary and important for His plan to be accomplished.

## Christians Are Identified With Christ in His Defeat of Satan

We can see this truth illustrated in the Lord's teaching about the vine and the branches. While it is true that no branch can bear fruit by itself; it must remain in the vine (John 15:4, NIV), it is also true that the vine does not bear fruit without the branches on which the fruit grows. This example shows us how God voluntarily limits Himself so that He not only needs the Church, but He cannot reach His chosen goal without her because of the design of His master plan.

Because of God's self-limitation, the Body is just as important as the Head for functioning, just as the branch is equally important as the vine for fruit bearing. *God limits Himself voluntarily for the purpose of making room for the members of His Bridehood to come into their full potential as generic (natural) sons of God.* God's goal in limiting Himself is to create a process by which His Church, as His legal equal, can grow more and more into the likeness of the Son. He desires to fulfill His plan to bring many sons to glory who will reach their highest potential as blood brothers of Christ Himself. God has taken us into His family as His very own, that is, as born again members of His household. He sees us differently from all other orders of beings, which are only created, not generated. *Through the new birth we are the next of kin.*

We are an organic, living part of Christ. As a part of Him, we took part in His total defeat of Satan and the forces of darkness before He arose from the dead. When He snatched the keys of death and hell from Satan and burst out of Hades, we shared in that victory. When He ascended to the heights of heaven and sat on His throne, we were raised up there with Him. Because Satan and all the demons of hell are beneath His feet, they are also under our feet. *When Christ defeated Satan it was our victory. He did not conquer Satan for Himself. The entire "substitutionary" work of Christ (taking our place) was for His Bride-elect, the Church.* He became flesh and blood so that He could take her place, enter the battle with Satan and overcome him as a perfect, sinless human being for her benefit, not for His. *Therefore, we are Satan's masters. He cannot lord it over us any longer.* His authority over us ended at Calvary. *Instead of him having power over us, we have been given authority over him.* This is the meaning of our place of honor on Christ's throne.

# Satan Still Uses Guerrilla Warfare

One of our greatest problems, after we understand who we really are, is that under satanic pressure we soon forget our identity. Satan knows what Christ did to him at Calvary and through the resurrection; though he realizes that, as a part of Christ, the believer is his master, he still carries on guerrilla warfare against the Church through the use of deception. Though guerrilla warfare is illegal, it is still warfare and must be faced and overcome. Why does God allow this? God could put Satan away completely, but He has chosen to use him to give the Church on-the-job training in winning the battle. We are in apprenticeship, preparing for our place with Christ on the throne after the Marriage Supper of the Lamb.

The crown belongs to the conqueror; without an enemy, we would have no practice in conquering. So, when God allows Satan to throw his black cape over our spirits, we are in danger of forgetting who we are. We are like the man James described who looks at his face in the mirror and then goes away and soon forgets what he looks like (James 1:23-24). Because we forget so easily that we have authority over Satan, we allow him to threaten us and beat us down. We forget we are really a part of Christ and Satan is under our authority. Without much thought, we fall back into our old life of fear and defeat, seeing ourselves as we were and not as we are now. We must constantly remind ourselves that we are in Christ; because Satan cannot touch Christ, he cannot touch us.[2]

Listen to this promise: "No one who has become a part of God's family makes a practice of sinning, for Christ, God's

Son, holds him securely, and the devil cannot get his hands on him" (1 John 5:18, TLB). Satan wants the believer to forget that he is risen and exalted with Christ and that his spirit is truly united with Christ on His throne with all enemies under his feet. If a Christian finds himself in bondage to demons of fear, sickness, disease, or limitation of any kind, it is only because he doesn't know or has forgotten who he really is and what Christ has done for him.

## Christians Need to Affirm Their True Identity

We always need to remind ourselves of our identity by affirming: "Because I am a part of Christ, accepted in the Beloved, I have the same place in the Father's heart as Jesus does. Because I am a part of Christ, the Father loves me as much as He loves Christ (John 17:23, 26). Because I am a part of Christ, I have His wisdom; He has become for us wisdom from God (1 Cor. 1:30, NIV). In the same way, I have His goodness. My goodness or righteousness is as good as His in the eyes of the Father because it is *His* righteousness. Because I am a living part of Christ, because Head and Body are one unit, *everything Christ is and has is also officially given to me.*"

*It is the Father's purpose to make all of the sons as closely like the Son as possible for the finite (the human) to be like the Infinite (God).* This kind of equality must be developed first in our character; then we can share in equality of rights, privileges, power and authority. God wants this to be a living reality, not just a legal or theoretical truth. "For all who are led by the Spirit of God are sons of God. And so we should not be like fearful, cringing slaves, but we should behave like God's very own children... and since we are his children, we will share his treasures — for all God gives to his son Jesus is now ours too. But if we are to share his glory, we must also share his suffering" (Rom. 8:14-17, TLB).

# The Unlimited Potential of the Church

All of this is assurance that it is God's intention for the Church to walk in the same life, power and divine freedom that Jesus walked in while He was on the earth. "As the Father hath sent me, *even so* send I you" (John 20:21). This "even so" suggests that we are sent under the same circumstances, with the same authority, and with the same resources as the Father sent the Son. *God does not set any arbitrary or chance limits to the Church's use of His resources.* Everything He has was made by Him and is available to His believing Church. "From his abundance we have all received one gracious blessing after another" (John 1:16, NLT). "May you experience the love of Christ, though it is too great to understand fully. Then you will be made complete with all the fullness of life and power that comes from God" (Eph. 3:19, NLT).

*All limitation is on the part of the believer.* One Old Testament saint, Enoch (Gen. 5:24), experienced the full blessing of walking with God, even to the point of being transported to heaven. What one man did by faith is possible for others to do. God has given us the keys of the kingdom of heaven, but He does not force us to use them. He waits. The rest is up to us, His Church. By His victory over Satan, He has given us the weapons we need. How well we use them is our responsibility and may even make a difference regarding our final rank or position in the corporate Bride of Christ.

# NOTES

1. When Jesus cried "It is finished," it was the end of the Mosaic covenant (an agreement of commandments and laws given to Moses by God for the nation of Israel) with its rules and laws, which He completely fulfilled: "Blotting out the handwriting of ordinances that was against us, which was contrary to us, and took it out of the way, nailing it to his cross. And, having spoiled principalities and powers [in his descent into hell], he made a show of them openly, triumphing over them in it" (Col. 2:14-15, KJV). Sin is basically a spiritual thing, a thing of the spirit; so, it must be dealt with in the realm of the spirit. If Jesus paid the full penalty of sin on the cross only — by His physical death alone — then sin is only a physical act. If sin is only a physical act, then every man could pay for his own sin by his own death. Yet, because sin is primarily in the spirit realm and of the spirit, Jesus' work was not finished when He gave up His physical life on the cross. It was not completed until He went into hell, paid once for all the eternal consequences of the combined sin of the world, completely defeated Satan and all his demons, arose victoriously from the dead, and carried His blood into the heavenly Holy of Holies and sprinkled it on the Mercy Seat (Ex. 26:34). Hallelujah!

2. Job 1:9-12 shows us that Satan cannot touch us, except by God's permission. He is entirely under God's control. Satan may have access to God's child only when God's divine love allows it. The end result, for the tested believer, is always twice as much blessing as before (Job. 42:10).

CHAPTER NUMBER

# 7

# The Mystery of Unanswered Prayer

*"This is the confidence we have in approaching God: that if we ask anything according to His will, he hears us. And if we know that he hears us — whatever we ask — we know that we have what we asked of him"* (1 John 5:14-15, NIV)

This scripture tells us that God the Father hearing our prayers is the same as answering them. It is a divinely inspired syllogism or logical deduction. When we ask in the will of God, it is logical that, since the request has come from God in the first place, He is even more interested in our receiving the answer than we are. The syllogism might go like this: *God has promised to hear and answer all prayers that are according to His will. My prayer is according to His will; therefore, He has answered my prayer.*

## Why?

In light of this and many other positive and clear promises to answer prayer, the question arises, *"Why* are some prayers apparently unanswered?" Satan has already been legally defeated, dethroned, disarmed, stripped of his weapons, and destroyed. The Church has actually been raised up and seated on the throne with Christ, with all enemies under her feet. If she has been given authority over all the power of the enemy and has been chosen by God to enforce His will on planet earth, *why* doesn't she do a better job living out the reality of her victory in Christ?

We have already seen that the Church — by her prayers and faith, as weak as they are — is the controlling factor in human affairs. she holds the balance of power, not only in the social order, but also in the salvation of individual people. Yet, we can see that she is not living up to her full spiritual potential as described in God's Word. Why is that? What is going wrong?

## God Is Hindered by Selfish Motives

Any reason for unanswered prayer is always on the human side. Most, if not all, Biblical writers take it for granted that all prayers, which are according to God's will, are answered. Neither Jesus nor the apostle John even hints at any such thing as unanswered prayer. "Ask, and it *will* be given to you; seek, and you *will* find; knock and it *will* be opened to you; for everyone who asks *receives*, and he who seeks *finds*; and to him who knocks it *will* be opened" (Matt. 7:7-8, NKJV). "And whatever you ask in My name, that I will do . . . .If you ask anything in My name I will do [it]" (John 14:13-14, NKJV). Take a look again at 1 John 5:14-15 quoted at beginning of the chapter.

In spite of these clear promises, we do have some references in the Word to unanswered prayer. While James mentions the fact of unanswered prayer, he clearly points out the reason is on the human side. "When you ask, you do not receive, because you ask with wrong motives, that you may spend what you get on your pleasures" (James 4:3, NIV).

## Paul's Prayer Was Not Answered

Paul describes an incident in his own life when his prayer was not answered, and he explains that the reason was on his side not God's. "Therefore, in order to keep me from becoming conceited [because of these surpassingly great revelations], I was given a thorn in my flesh, a messenger of Satan, to torment me" (2 Cor. 12:7, NIV). Paul also tells us he asked the Lord three times to take the "thorn" away but his prayer was not answered. The Lord refused, and for a good reason.

Although this is the only situation like this in the New Testament, it may paint a picture of a principle that applies to almost everyone. Pride is probably the most dangerous and deadly of all sins. It caused the downfall of Lucifer (Satan), with all the tragedies connected to it. It brought the original earth to utter confusion, and covered it in gloomy darkness. It upset the balance of the whole planet. For any created being to make itself the center of the world rather than God is disastrous and self-destructive. Satan, who was once Lucifer, makes this plain.

Before his fall, Lucifer was the highest of all beings created before Adam. According to Isaiah 14 and Ezekiel 28 he was the guardian of the very throne of God, the anointed cherub who covers, full of wisdom and perfect in beauty (NKJV). Ezekiel tells us Lucifer was next to God Himself and that his heart was filled with pride because of his beauty. He also grew proud of his great splendor and brilliance, and his God-given wisdom became perverted. Verse 18 in *The Living Bible* reads: "You defiled your holiness with lust for gain; therefore I brought forth fire from your own actions and let it burn you to ashes." His strong cravings and greed, his ambition for power, were so set on fire by the exceptional gifts God had showered on him that his personality actually broke down and fell apart. The inner fires ignited by his conceit and self-worship burned him to ashes. *This is the common pattern of self-destruction.*

Paul recognized this danger when he warned young Timothy that a bishop (overseer) must not be a novice or new convert "in case he becomes conceited and incurs the doom passed on the devil" (1 Tim. 3:6, *Moffatt*). Yes, Satan tries to produce the Lucifer syndrome in every believer because he knows it will bring on him what Paul calls "the condemnation of the devil" (1 Tim. 3:6). What does Paul mean? Paul understood conceit is always from the devil and is one of his most devastating tools. He experienced this first hand when an abundance of revelations given to him put him in danger of becoming conceited. To counteract this danger of extreme pride and the chance of falling into the condemnation of the devil, Paul says, "I was given a thorn in my flesh, a messenger from Satan to torment me and keep me from becoming proud" (2 Cor. 12:7, NLT). Further, as a safety measure to protect him, God denied his prayer that the thorn be removed.

## God Is Hindered by Spiritual Pride

It is true that Paul's experience was a one-of-a-kind

event, but the lesson regarding dealing with pride applies to everyone. Very few people can handle praise and kudos, either from others or from God, without becoming a little conceited. What Christian hasn't experienced the subtle temptation to swell up with pride even over the simplest compliment? How many times have we given a testimony about answered prayer in a way designed to make ourselves look good with an added "to God be the glory"? Our human ego or personality is so swollen with pride since Adam's fall that we are easy targets for Satan and his demons. C. S. Lovett said they lurk constantly just outside our skin, and they take advantage of even the smallest opportunity to make us feel proud of ourselves.

Who can imagine how much God would do for His children if He weren't concerned with their strong tendency to become proud? Even if we don't brag aloud after we've done well as a speaker or given a testimony of answered prayer or been used by God to express some spiritual gift or special grace, we are tempted to relish secretly the attention we received. If it were not for God's help during moments like these, we would easily fall into Satan's trap of self conceit. God knows most of us are weak when it comes to this temptation, so He is very careful not to honor many publically when it comes to miraculous answers to prayer.

This does not mean that God turns His back on us or His promise to answer prayers for the miraculous, when they are requested. Rather, it is human weakness that frustrates Him and keeps back the answer that is ready and waiting. If God felt it was necessary to refuse Paul's prayer for relief from the "thorn," so that he wouldn't become proud of his revelations from God, could this also explain why God cannot answer more prayers for the rest of His children?

Sadly, it is true that the sands of time are cluttered with the debris of broken lives of many who were once greatly used by God, but were crushed on the rocks of spiritual pride. Author and minister Watchman Nee helps us understand when he says God's great work is to reduce us, that is, our ego or self-importance. Until God has done a work of true humility and brokenness in His servants, He is unable to answer some of our prayers. If He did answer, He would take the risk of producing in us that kind of pride that goes before a fall. If God could trust us to stay humble, just think how many more answers to prayer He could freely give us.

This principle may also explain why answers to prayer for healing sometimes are not received. If the answer to prayer for healing in Paul's case was dangerous to him, how much more so might it be to many others? Though no one since Paul has ever had as much reason to be exalted because of the abundance of revelations, very few have his ability to stay humble. Do you think it's possible that one reason some people are not healed is because God sees they might become swollen with spiritual pride and then fall into the condemnation of the devil? If God thought it best not to answer Paul's prayer for healing in order to keep him humble, can't this also explain why some other prayers for healing are not answered?

## God Is Hindered by Prayerlessness

Let's take a look at another reason for unanswered prayer. In previous chapters we have examined the fact that the authority, which Christ gave to His Church to rule over Satan and his demons, works only in the system of believing prayer, which God set in order. By God's own choice, all of this far-reaching, given authority is completely useless without the prayers of a believing Church. *If the Church does not pray, God will not act.* Why? If He acted without the Church, He would cancel His plan to make her ready for rulership through on-the-job training in enforcing Christ's victory at Calvary. If He had not decided to bring the Church to full maturity as His co-ruler, God would not have put in place the system of prayer in the first place.

Prayer, all by itself, possesses no built-in power. On the contrary, prayer is an actual admission of need and helplessness. If God chose, He could act on a whim without regard to prayer or the lack of prayer. All power comes first from God and belongs to Him alone. *He chose prayer, not simply as a way to get things done for Himself, but as part of the teaching program for getting the Church ready for her royal work, which will take place after the Marriage Supper of the Lamb. Unless she understands this and gives herself sincerely to God's plan of prayer, the power needed to overcome and restrain Satan on earth will not be released.*

God has the power to overcome Satan without the help of His Church through prayer and faith. Yet, if He overcame Satan without her, she would be robbed of the enforcement practice needed to help her gain spiritual strength in overcoming. This is God's number one reason for creating the system of prayer and purposely committing Himself to answer. *Thus, we can say no authority exists without the tireless, continual prayer of the Church.*

# We Are Great Organizers, But Poor Pray-ers

If the Church does not realize the importance of her role in prayer and intercession for others, she ties God's hands and gives up her right to answered prayer. This brings us to the greatest reason for the shortage of answered prayer: *prayerlessness* itself. "You do not have, because you do not ask God" (James 4:2, NIV). We pointed out earlier that our social order has been preserved from total decay, though just a few have prayed very few prayers. The Church's lack of prayer is well-known. We all stand convicted of our personal lack of prayer. The days of intercessors like David Brainerd, Praying Hyde, Father Nash, E. M. Bounds, etc., seem to be gone. In many cases, the Western Church has lost her prayer stamina and her mission churches have outdone her — like those in Asia, Africa, South America, Indonesia, and those underground churches in oppressed countries. Yes, we are great organizers but poor pray-ers. *Our lack of prayer is one of the main reasons for so few answers.*

# Are We Operating Church Treadmills?

The average local church provides great Sunday school and educational programs, as well as youth programs, social activities and spiritual retreats for all ages. Many churches launch wonderful evangelistic campaigns, featuring big-name celebrities and the latest in Christian entertainment. Many also have a well-structured, efficient financial program. All in all, things may work smoothly and in high gear. These programs may all be well and good, *but if they are substitutes for a powerful prayer program, they may be useless as far as damaging Satan's kingdom is concerned.*

A church without an intelligent, well-organized and systematic prayer program is simply operating a religious treadmill. We pray this is not a common description of most of our churches today. I wonder if we could see what God sees, if we would see an amazing forest of giant church treadmills operating in full swing all over the United States and in other parts of the world. Such a movement might be very exhilarating. It might involve huge numbers of employees, take great amounts of time and demand an enormous financial budget. It might even convince us of its success. It definitely might flatter the ego. *But any church program, no matter how impressive, is not much more than a church treadmill if it is not supported by enough prayer.* It is doing almost nothing to damage Satan's kingdom.

## Prayer Is Where the Action Is

If our theology of prayer is scriptural, then PRAYER IS WHERE THE ACTION IS. Evangelist John Wesley was right when he said, "God does nothing but in answer to prayer." So was S.D. Gordon when he said, "Prayer is striking the winning blow....Service is gathering up the results." And E.M. Bounds was also right when he said, "God shapes the world by prayer. The prayers of God's saints are the capital stock of heaven by which God carries on His great work upon earth." I once doubted these claims. Only when I started to understand better the deeper aspects of the theology of prayer was I convinced of their truth. Since these claims are true, surely prayer is where the action is.

# Israel and Amalek

The Old Testament story of the battle between Israel and Amalek draws a verbal picture of this important truth regarding prayer. God brought the nation of Israel out of Egypt and was leading the people toward the Promised Land for the purpose of making them into the Messianic nation (the nation that would give birth to Christ, the Messiah). Satan, the great enemy of God and His Messianic program, tried to stop Israel's progress toward the land. He stirred up the ungodly nation of Amalek, a descendant of Ishmael, using the Amalekites as a means to oppose and fight Israel.

As the battle began, "Moses said to Joshua, 'Choose some of our men and go out to fight the Amalekites. Tomorrow I will stand on top of the hill with the staff of God in my hands.' So Joshua fought the Amalekites as Moses had ordered, and Moses, Aaron and Hur went to the top of the hill. As long as Moses held up his hands, the Israelites were winning, but whenever he lowered his hands, the Amalekites were winning" (Ex. 17:9-11, NIV). You know the rest of the story. When Moses got tired and had to rest his arms, Aaron and Hur stood on either side and supported him until Amalek was completely beaten and God's plan for the Messianic nation continued.

# Victory on Top of the Hill

To the casual onlooker, all the action was taking place on the battlefield where the troops were in combat, but the spiritually sensitive person will recognize the battle was fought, and the victory was won, on top of the hill where

Moses, Aaron and Hur together held up the staff, which was the symbol of God's power. The Amalekites were simply the tools of Satan. They were controlled and motivated by demonic forces. When the three men on the top of the hill joined in believing prayer, the demonic forces influencing the Amalekites were stopped and the troops paralyzed. Then Israel emerged victorious.

When tiredness forced Moses to rest, the evil spirits started up again and energized Israel's enemies. That's why Moses needed Aaron and Hur to hold up his hands. It worked. They helped Moses by holding up his hands in prayer until the sun went down. Then, it is said, Joshua completely overpowered Amalek, but the *real* action was on the top of the hill. There the demonic spirits were stopped in their tracks so Joshua could win the battle. The winning blow was struck on the hill of intercession. Joshua and Israel merely gathered up the results. Truly, prayer *is* where the action is.

Since this is true, prayer becomes the Christian's greatest privilege. Why? Prayer places the intercessor on the front line of spiritual battle and conquest. Intercessors share equally in the ongoing spiritual struggle against demonic forces with pastors, evangelists, missionaries, or any other soldier of the cross. In addition, the spiritual weapons available to them are just as effective as those used by the most powerful spiritual leaders.

As S.D. Gordon said, "Prayer puts one in touch with a planet. I can as really be touching hearts for God in far away India or China through prayer as though I were there. A man may go aside today, and shut his door, and as really spend a half hour in India for God . . . as though he were there in person" (*Quiet Talks On Prayer*). In other words, prayer is not limited by location. This is why Christian author Alexander Maclaren said, in speaking of the mission field, that much prayer for those on the field by those at the home base means power released on the field, and that weakness at home means weakness on the field.

## Prayer — Not Personality, Talent, Skillful Preaching, or Art

Does anyone even imagine that people are set free from Satan's power by human talent, by someone's personality or charm, by smooth persuasive speech, or by the magic of Hollywood techniques? God may use all of these gifts, but they have no power, by themselves, to save even one person from slavery to sin. The apostle John reminds us, "human effort accomplishes nothing" (John 6:63, NLT).

*From heaven's standpoint, all spiritual victories are won, not primarily through a pastor's sermon, not primarily in the glamorous light of publicity, nor yet through the showy blaring of trumpets and musical instruments, but in the secret place of prayer.* The only power that overcomes Satan and frees people from his stranglehold is the power of the Holy Spirit; the only power that releases the energy of the Holy Spirit is *the power of believing prayer.*

Thank God for the gifts, talents and preaching ability of men like Evangelist Billy Graham, but the power that has changed the lives of thousands through Billy Graham's ministry is not the power of superior gifts, unusual talents, clever speech or persuasive techniques, but the power released by the prayer and faith of the millions of his prayer helpers. From heaven's point of view, the combined prayer and intercession which has supported Billy Graham is the real reason for his success in reaching people for Christ and continues to be the reason for the success of his son Franklin Graham. Because of the huge program of prayer warfare on their behalf, Satan's forces attacking their efforts are overcome and stopped in the same way they were when Moses, Aaron and Hur interceded for Joshua and Israel against Amalek.

The spiritual power of the message of preachers, radio and television hosts, etc., is not first of all their superior talents and skills or even the truth of their message — although these are important. *Instead, the power that stops Satan's attacks and changes the hearts of people is released only by serious, believing prayer.*

The same may be said about the message of a Christian book. The art and skill of the author are important, but the message is hidden unless the Holy Spirit opens and instructs the minds of the readers. Again we see that prayer is the secret power, because PRAYER IS WHERE THE ACTION IS.

## Prayer and Reward

Some people are saddened when, for some reason, they are unable to serve God on a foreign mission field or perhaps in another full-time ministry position. *Yet, through the faithful work of prayer, they may accomplish as much and win just as great a reward as if they had been on that mission field or in that ministry position in person.* Those who grieve because they feel they have no shining gifts or awesome talents or are not able to minister because of age or sickness, may — through faithful intercession — also share in the heavenly reward just as those who are highly gifted. Why is this so? It is because PRAYER IS WHERE THE ACTION IS. "Anyone who receives a prophet because he is a prophet will receive a prophet's reward, and anyone who receives a righteous man because he is a righteous man will receive a righteous man's reward" (Matt. 10:41, NIV). If simple hospitality and kindness bring equal rewards, then surely a prayer support ministry will also be rewarded.

## No Room for Self-pity

This leaves no room for feeling sorry for yourself or for jealousy of people more gifted than you, that is, if you are willing to take your place as a prayer warrior. *In heaven's book, the overlooked, nameless Christian in the most far away place is just as important and — if he is faithful — will receive just as great a reward as the most beautiful, talented and popular leader. Hallelujah!* Yes, it's true that all the faithful prayer warriors are at the front lines making a great contribution in the battle as much as the bold, well-known leaders. They will share equally in the reward. This is a true saying: "The fate of the world is in the hands of nameless saints."

## Daniel's Intercession

Chapter ten of the book of Daniel gives us another picture of this truth. Again, the mission of the Messianic nation Israel was in view. The vision of the future of this nation came to

Daniel at the end of a three-week stretch of fasting. During that whole three weeks Daniel was grieving for his people; that is, he poured out his heart in prayer concerning the future of Israel. At last, the angel came with the message from heaven and shared with Daniel the amazing reason he had taken so long to arrive.

It seems Daniel's prayer was heard in heaven the very day he began to pray and immediately this heavenly messenger was sent out to bring him the answer, but the angel was intercepted. *The Living Bible* says it this way: "That very day I was sent here to meet you. But for twenty-one days the mighty Evil Spirit who overrules the kingdom of Persia blocked my way. Then Michael, one of the top officers of the heavenly army, came to help me, so that I was able to break through these spirit rulers of Persia" (Dan. 10:12-13).

## Battle in the Spirit World

This is an actual historical account of a literal struggle in the unseen world. It's no doubt an example of many similar conflicts that rage constantly in the spirit world. It is the story of an action on two levels. Down by the river is a man in fasting and prayer. He labors, he pleads, he insists, he persists, he requests, he wrestles, and he agonizes. He grieves day after day. He has read the prophet Jeremiah's prophecy about the 70 years of captivity and knows the time is almost up. It's almost time for the words of the prophecy to come true.

Now we know that God is sovereign and could, if He chose, fulfill His prophecies without any help. But Daniel evidently understood that prayer had a part to play in making the words of the prophecy actually happen. God had made the prophecy in the first place, *but when it was time for the prophecy's fulfillment, He did not fulfill it randomly outside His program of prayer. He looked for a man whose heart could carry the burden of intercession.* Prayer for others is the most unselfish thing anyone can do.

As always, God made the decision in heaven. A man was called *to enforce that decision on earth through faith and prayer.* This part of the struggle — the prayer sessions by the river — was on an observable level, but another part of the battle was invisible from earth. While Daniel was on his face praying, a parallel conflict — a related battle — was erupting in the heavens. Two angels, and possibly the spirit forces under their command, were engaged in violent combat that kept going for three weeks.

Since God does nothing except in answer to prayer, if Daniel had grown tired and discouraged, God would have had to find someone else to intercede or else allow his angelic messenger to be defeated. Though the answer to his prayer was already given and on its way, if Daniel had given up, it most likely would have never arrived. Therefore, the real battle was fought and the victory won in that place of prayer; the action that really counted was on the riverbank.

## Why Urgent Prayer Is Crucial

This story about Daniel's prayer experience suggests an enlightening principle, which may explain why some prayers don't seem to get answered. Since the promise in 1 John 5 is true, every prayer offered in faith according to God's will is always answered in heaven, but Satan never allows an answer to reach earth if he can help it. *Persistence and importunity (urgent request) in prayer are not needed to persuade a willing God but to enable Him to overcome opposition of hindering evil spirits.* If God's purpose in His prayer program is to give us on-the-job training in overcoming Satan, He cannot — at random — get rid of demonic hindrances. If He went over the Church's head, took the matter out of her hands, and won the victory for her, it would keep her from growing into full maturity and readiness for the throne as an overcomer. *This is the reason for the Biblical teaching on the importance of persistent, urgent prayer (importunity).*

It is possible the answer to many prayers that have already been approved in heaven may never be received because the one praying gets tired, discouraged or frightened, and gives up the fight. Jesus tells us that the man who needed three loaves of bread from his neighbor got them because he kept asking. Then He adds: "Ask and keep on asking and it shall be given you; seek and keep on seeking and you shall find; knock and keep on knocking and the door shall be opened to you" (Luke 11:9, *Amplified*). The word from God to Habakkuk the prophet also applies here: " ... the vision has its own appointed hour, it ripens, it will flower; if it be long then wait, for it is sure, and it will not be late" (Hab. 2:3, *Moffatt*). *One reason many prayers are apparently not answered is the failure of the one praying to keep on praying with urgency until the answer comes.*

Listen to what S.D. Gordon says about this in his *Quiet Talks On Prayer*: "It is a fiercely contested conflict. Satan is a trained strategist, and an obstinate fighter. He refuses to acknowledge defeat until he must. It is the fight for his life....The enemy yields only what he must. He yields only what is taken. Therefore, the ground must be taken step by step....He continually renews his attacks, therefore the ground taken must be held against him in the VICTOR'S Name." "Therefore put on the full armor of God, so that when the day of evil comes, you may be able to stand your ground, and after you have done everything, to stand. Stand firm then, with the belt of truth buckled around your waist, with the breastplate of righteousness [integrity] in place" (Eph. 6:13-14, NIV). *This is a conflict of wills.* If Satan's will, persistence and determination lasts longer than that of the one praying, the intercessor is beaten. Yet, the intercessor has the advantage because of Christ's victory and never needs to lose. *Persistent prayer combined with strong faith is unbeatable.*

## What Is the Cause of Prayerlessness?

With such promises of victory, why do Christians not take time to pray? So far we have looked at prayerlessness and the lack of persistent prayer as reasons for prayer not being productive. Yet, in light of God's many clear promises to answer prayer, this question arises: *Why* is the prayer activity of the Church so sadly neglected and put aside? What is the reason for the Church's lack of prayer? Many reasons could be mentioned but perhaps the most basic reason is LACK OF FAITH IN THE GOODNESS AND HONOR OF THE WORD OF GOD. "Ask and it will be given to you; seek and you *will* find; knock and the door will be opened to you" (Matt. 7:7, NIV). If the Church were truly convinced that such promises would be fulfilled, prayer would be the main business of her daily life. *Lack of faith that God will actually carry out His Word is the first great cause for not praying.* This unbelief is so much a part of us it has become an automatic response and is the cause behind the weak prayer life of the Church.

## We Need a True Evaluation of God's Word

Today, we need a true evaluation, a proper analysis of God's Word. According to author Erich Sauer in *The King of the Earth*, man's spiritual nature expresses itself mainly in his power of speech. "Speech is the direct self-revelation of the inward man or of the personality. Thought is, as it were, the inward speech of the spirit and the spoken or written word forms a body for the thought. Speech is the instrument for the manifestation of the spirit." Your thought is you! Listen to Proverbs 23:7: *"For as he thinks in his heart so [is] he"* (NKJV). *If thought is such a necessary part of the person, as this scripture teaches, then speech — because it is the body or collection of our thoughts — must be important as well. Therefore, God's Word must truly be a part of Himself; God Himself actually lives in His Word.*

We do need to recognize, of course, that in the most basic sense, Jesus Christ is the Word. He is the eternal Word who was with the Father in the beginning (John 1:1). He is described as the *Logos* or Word because it is He who perfectly shows us the Father. "No one has ever seen God. But the unique One [Jesus], who is himself God, is near to the Father's heart. He has revealed God to us" (John 1:18, NLT).

Today, we do not have the eternal Word living among

us as a human being, but we do have His counterpart, the Holy Spirit, who is called the Comforter (John 16:7, KJV). It is the Holy Spirit who inspired the written revelation of God's nature and His actions, which we have in our hands today and know as the Bible. "All Scripture is inspired by God and is useful to teach us what is true and to make us realize what is wrong in our lives. It corrects us when we are wrong and teaches us to do what is right. God uses it to prepare and equip his people to do every good work" (2 Tim. 3:16-17, NLT). Though God used men of good character to do the actual writing, that which is written is truly the Word of God. This written Word of God forms a body for the thoughts of God. The written Word is not just words, but is given life by God's divine breath. The Word is *alive* (Heb. 4:12); it is God appearing, actually coming into sight. The Word is a body for the Holy Spirit. In this sense, it is truly a part of God Himself; God actually lives in His Word.

*The written Word is taking Jesus' place today.* It is full of His personality and His true character. *Since the words of Jesus are actually a part of Him, all the power and authority that He has are also part of His written Word.* The written Word carries the same authority as the words Jesus spoke when He was on earth. *This living Word — spoken by Christians full of faith, not mixed with doubt, but with pure hearts that make no room for Satan — carries the same authority as when spoken by the Lord Jesus Himself.* If it weren't for the Church's chronic unbelief, she would be acting on this truth all the time. We thank God for the contemporary examples of this kind of powerful faith given to us by those who truly believe.[1]

God is both the author and power source of the Word. You cannot separate God from His Word. This is why Jesus could say, ". . . the scripture cannot be broken" (John 10:35, KJV). Because Scripture is God-breathed, it cannot fail without taking God off His throne. If God could not carry out His own word, which comes out of His mouth, He would not be God.

## There Is a Cure for Prayerlessness

Since the things we've just discussed are true, the warning against "Bibliolatry" by some so-called Bible scholars is not necessary. Some of them claim that too much reverence for the Bible as the inerrant (infallible or faultless) Word of God is a form of idolatry or idol worship. Yet, in light of what God Himself says about His Word, can this be possible? Look at these Scriptures: "God is not a man, that he should lie, nor a son of man, that he should change his mind. Does he speak and then not act? Does he promise and not fulfill?" (Numbers 23:19, NIV). "I watch over my word to perform it" (Jer. 1:12, ASV). Further, the writer of the letter to the Hebrews tells us it is impossible for God to lie (Heb. 6:18, NIV). In John 10:35, Jesus Himself states clearly "the scripture *cannot* be broken" (KJV). He also confirmed the accuracy of the Scriptures when He said to the Jews, "They testify of me" (John 5:39, NKJV). He Himself stood up for their honor when He said, "Your word is truth" (John 17:17, NKJV).

We can see God's own reverence for His Word in Psalm 138:2: "For You have magnified Your word above all Your name" (NKJV). We may not truly understand the meaning of this verse but we have to admit it shows us God's strong commitment to His Word. God's honor is forever joined with

His Word. *If the Church would truly believe in the honor and integrity of God's Word, her lack of prayer would be cured.*

## The Success of Mature and Perfect Faith

*In light of all this, we can say that prayer which seems to not be answered — referring to prayer according to God's will — may be explained by Satan's deception, bluff and opposition, plus the believer's blindness, ignorance, fear, personal character flaws, and the failure to keep asking and believing with unchanging faith.* Since God is God, we cannot lay the responsibility for unanswered prayer at heaven's door. Remember these scriptural truths: "Let God be true, but every man a liar" (Rom. 3:4). "God that cannot lie" (Titus 1:2). "The Scripture cannot be broken" (John 10:35). We must no longer cast doubt on the honor of God's Word. *Faith will never be perfected and come to maturity until we accept our responsibility for failure. The mystery of unanswered prayer is failure on the human side alone.*

Late 19th century preacher and writer Alexander Maclaren says that if we understood ourselves better, and could see as God sees, we would trace all of our unanswered prayers to problems with our own Christian character. What can we do to change this? As believers in Christ, we must keep on seeking God with all our heart, doing our best to obey His will and walk in the light and understanding He gives us. If we do this, we can know for certain God is maturing our faith and that we will receive the answers for which we have prayed.

As long as answers to prayer are delayed, we can be sure our faith is not quite what it should be, since Jesus says, "Because of your faith, it will happen" (Matt. 9:29, NLT), and,

"I tell you the truth, if you have faith and don't doubt, you can do things like this and much more. You can even say to this mountain, 'May you be lifted up and thrown into the sea,' and it will happen" (Matt. 21:21, NLT). He says further, "I tell you, you can pray for anything, and if you believe that you've received it, it will be yours" (Mark 11:24, NLT), and, "Anything is possible if a person believes" (Mark 9:23, NLT).

We can draw the conclusion that *Jesus clearly does not allow for any such thing as unanswered prayer.* Many things may keep us from developing a mature faith, but *when faith is perfected the answer also is received.* We can say this is a dependable law of God. *Yes, the mystery of unanswered prayer is explained by human failure alone, and in the end by the failure of immature and imperfect faith.*

# NOTES

1. One example in the 20<sup>th</sup> century (1965) is the revival that began on the Indonesian island of Timor. Controversy surrounds reports of this revival and some competent observers feel that events have been greatly blown out of proportion. Others insist that almost every miracle experienced in the first century Church has been repeated among these people who were simple enough to believe and doubt not. According to eyewitnesses, some who were unable to read or write became the ones used to *reproduce* the most amazing of the Biblically recorded miracles. This certainly goes along with the words of Jesus, "I praise you, Father, Lord of heaven and earth, because you have hidden these things from the wise and learned, and revealed them to little children" (Luke 10:21, NIV). I wonder what blessing we might be losing because of our religious pride, which shuts down true faith!

# 8

# The Problem of Faith

*"Jesus said to him, 'If you can believe, all things [are] possible to him who believes.'"* (Mark 9:23, NKJV)

T he problem of keeping a strong living faith, a faith without any doubt, is a very real challenge. Even those who have daily devotional habits of prayer and intercession often doubt whether their prayers are being heard. In fact, it seems this is the case for a large part of the body of Christ. Well-organized prayer programs can be crippled easily by a lack of truly victorious faith. Since very few Christians know how to cling to this achieving faith, many prayer efforts bog down in frustration and defeat. *How can we solve this problem?*

## Praise Is the Answer

We've had a lot of teaching on prayer, but until recently we've had little instruction in praise. Yet, the Bible emphasizes praise much more than prayer. In the Bible, the whole universe, both living things and inanimate things, is pictured as one huge chorus of praise to the Creator. Notice especially Psalms 148-150. And Psalm 145:10 tells us, "All Your works shall praise You" (NKJV). *Praise is the all-consuming activity of angels. Heaven is one great song of praise.* Cherubim and seraphim (angelic beings) never stop adoring Him. "Each of these living beings had six wings, and their wings were covered all over with eyes, inside and out. Day after day and night after night they keep on saying, 'Holy, holy, holy is the Lord God, the Almighty — the one who always was, who is, and who is still to come" (Rev. 4:8, NLT).

Listen to John's further description: "Then I looked again, and I heard the voices of thousands and millions of angels around the throne and of the living beings and the elders. And they sang in a mighty chorus: 'Worthy is the Lamb who was slaughtered — to receive power and riches and wisdom and strength and honor and glory and blessing'" (Rev. 5:11-12, NLT). And again, "Then I heard again what sounded like the shout of a vast crowd or the roar of mighty ocean waves or the crash of loud thunder: 'Praise the LORD! For the Lord our God, the Almighty, reigns'" (Rev. 19:6, NLT). Doesn't it make sense that if all of heaven's time and energy are taken up with praise, our time and energy on earth should be full of praise as well?

## Praise Is Practical

For some reason most Christians don't understand the great importance of praise. Many think praise is a beautiful thing to do, but that it doesn't really have any practical value. But think about it. If praise is the most important activity of angels, a good reason for praise must exist. If heaven believes it is important to keep their songs of praise going day and night and never stopping (Rev. 4:8), then praise must be extremely powerful. Furthermore, can you imagine God allowing all this to go on in heaven if it were pointless and made no sense? No, of course not! It's time to take a look at some of the practical aspects of praise.

## Praise Develops Good Character

If the most important thing angels do in heaven is praise, it only stands to reason that praise is also the most important thing human beings can do on earth. Praise is the highest activity of the human spirit. The greatest goal of all creation is to become more and more like the good and beautiful Creator God. This is the highest good, the greatest joy, the most delightful pathway the human spirit can travel. Just as hate, hostility and cursing against God strengthens what is most vile, devilish and mean in the human spirit, so worship and praise of the infinitely lovely God reinforces and strengthens all that is most noble, unselfish and good in our inner person.

As one worships and praises, he is changed step by step, from one level of glory to the next, into the likeness of the eternally happy God. This wonderful process will continue forever and ever. Praise is God's most useful tool in accomplishing His greatest goal: bringing many sons to glory — restoring His children to the likeness and character of Christ Himself.

## Praise Is Good for Mental Health

The subject of mental health among Christians receives a lot of attention these days. In the world at large, it is claimed over half of the available hospital beds are taken by patients with mental or nervous disorders. In order to deal with this problem through the years, huge mental health facilities have been built and the profession of psychiatry has been developed. It is my belief that a massive program of individual and group praise could put a large number of psychiatrists out of business and close down many mental institutions.

All of our mental and nervous disorders can be summed up in this one thing: too much concern over our personal ego, namely, self-centeredness. When the personality becomes centered on itself, it disintegrates or breaks apart. Out of extreme self-centeredness arise self-defense, anger and aggressive antisocial behavior. According to psychiatrists, these are the symptoms of mental sickness, which make it necessary for a person to be hospitalized. To make oneself the center of life is self-destructive. Jesus talked about this truth when He said, "If you try to hang on to your life, you will lose it. But if you give up your life for my sake, you will save it" (Luke 9:24, NLT).

## Praise Takes Self off the Throne

One of the greatest values of praise is this: it decentralizes the self. Praise takes self off the throne of a person's life. Worship and praise of God makes a drastic change in our lives. Praise demands a shift of center from self to God. A person cannot praise without giving up his over concern with himself. When praise becomes a way of life our kind, merciful and eternally loving God becomes the center of our lives rather than our weak and broken self. Then our personality becomes properly blended and put together, and stresses and strains disappear. This results in mental wholeness. Praise actually produces a kind of forgetfulness of self; forgetting self produces mental health.

## Praise Costs Less

A person may pay a very expensive fee per hour to a psychiatrist to listen and look wise, and yet come away even weaker and certainly no better. But when a born-again follower of Christ suffering with depression and other emotional stresses turns to our wise and loving God in praise, a healing process begins. Yes, praise is much more than an empty, religious form or ritual. It is the most practical and rewarding activity in which a Christian can partake.

## Praise Brings Peace to Our Homes

Praise can make a difference in our homes where stresses and strains are most likely to take place. Nothing like praise can rid the soul of self-pity, defensiveness and hostility. Praise and household problems cannot exist together. A person cannot praise and sulk at the same time. Praise and irritation cannot be in the same place at the same time. A consistent plan of personal praise could make a marriage counselor unnecessary and could no doubt reduce the number of cases in the divorce courts.

## A Biblical Example of the Power of Praise

For many reasons, praise is important; much more is said in the Bible about praise than about prayer. *For some reason, Satan is even more afraid of praise than he is of prayer.* A powerful example is given to us in 2 Chronicles 20. It seems a group united in their hostility — Moab, Ammon, and the people of Mt. Seir — declared war on Jehoshaphat, king of Judah. Right away, the king called the nation to repentance, fasting and prayer. People from all across the nation came together in Jerusalem for a great prayer meeting. Because of this, God spoke to Jehoshaphat and the nation through Jahaziel the prophet and assured them they would win a victory without a battle.

This situation is described in 2 Chronicles 20:20-22: "Early the next morning the army of Judah went out into the wilderness of Tekoa. On the way Jehoshaphat stopped and said, 'Listen to me, all you people of Judah and Jerusalem! Believe in the LORD your God, and you will be able to stand firm. Believe in his prophets, and you will succeed.' After consulting the people, the king appointed singers to walk ahead of the army, singing to the LORD and praising him for his holy splendor. This is what they sang: 'Give thanks to the LORD; his faithful love endures forever!' At the very moment they began to sing and give praise, the LORD caused the armies of Ammon, Moab, and Mount Seir to start fighting among themselves" (NLT).

## An Army Commits Suicide

Why do you think praise worked so well in this situation? *It is because this was a spiritual battle, a conflict between unseen spirits.* Since Judah was the Messianic nation, Satan had driven this hostile group of nations to wipe out Judah in an attempt to keep the Messiah (Christ) from coming. But Jehoshaphat's prayer-and-praise program was more destructive to the enemy than a battle waged with deadly weapons.

The nationwide program of fasting and prayer, along with the praise of the choir and the Lord's hidden attack plan, completely confused the evil spirits controlling Judah's enemies. The opposing armies became disoriented and hysterical, falling into uncontrollable panic. In this state of mind, they began fighting each other until they totally crushed themselves. The entire hostile army committed suicide.

## Why Is Praise So Powerful Against Satan?

Mrs. Frances Metcalf points out something very interesting in her little book, *Making His Praise Glorious*. She shows us Bible verses that tell us God's living space is between the cherubim (Psalm 80:1, 99:1, and Isaiah 37:16). We know these passages are talking about the cherubim figures covering Israel's sacred Ark of the Covenant; and we know they are earthly symbols of what is real in heaven. They take their meaning from the cherubim (angelic beings) which are around God's throne, who never rest day or night as they declare, "Holy, holy, holy, Lord God Almighty."

God lives in an aura, in an atmosphere, in the very surroundings of praise. Praise and God's presence are on the same wavelength; they attract one another. Though God is everywhere at once, He is not necessarily everywhere in benign influence. Where joyful, happy praise is expressed, God is powerfully and compassionately active. In Psalm 22:3 we are told God inhabits the praises of His people. Wherever God is adored, loved, worshipped, and praised He will openly reveal Himself through His living, dynamic presence.

Keep in mind, *God's presence always gets rid of Satan*. Satan cannot carry on his activities in God's divine environment. For years, many people have known that *praise is power* without completely understanding why. Isn't this a good explanation? Isn't it a good reason to praise God all the time? In short, *Satan is allergic to praise; so, where there is massive, victorious praise, Satan is paralyzed, tied up and driven out.*[1]

The secret, then, to a victorious, overcoming faith is *praise.* It was the apostle James who said, "Resist the devil, and he will flee from you" (Jas. 4:7). Because praise creates the environment which God enjoys, it becomes the most powerful protection against Satan and his attacks. Since praise is hated so much by Satan, it becomes the greatest defense, the most destructive weapon we can use in our battle against him. *Praise guarantees victory* in prayer because it overcomes Satan, who is our greatest enemy in prayer warfare.

## The Importance of Continuous Massive Praise

The kind of praise that defeats the devil is not just a once-in-a-while praise, or a praise that changes with mood swings or circumstances. *It is continuous praise, praise that goes on all the time, praise that is a way of life.* "I will praise the LORD *at all times.* I will *constantly* speak his praises" (Psalm 34:1, NLT). "What joy for those who can live in your house, *always singing your praises*" (Psalm 84:4, NLT). Praise is the atmosphere of heaven. In fact, praise is so important in heaven, a whole group of created beings totally give themselves to praising God: "Each of these living beings had six wings, and their wings were covered all over with eyes, inside and out. Day after day and night after night they keep on saying, 'Holy, holy, holy is the Lord God, the

Almighty — the one who always was, who is, and who is still to come'" (Rev. 4:8, NLT).

In a similar way, God showed King David the importance and power of praise on earth. Following the heavenly pattern, King David chose and set aside a huge group of 4,000 Levites whose only job was to praise the Lord (1 Chron. 23:5). They did nothing else. One of King David's last official acts before his death was the organization of a set program of praise. It looked like this: Each morning and each night a smaller group among the 4,000 took part in a praise service. "And each morning and evening they stood before the LORD to sing songs of thanks and praise to him" (1 Chron. 23:30, NLT). Sadly — to the shame and defeat of the Church — the importance of massive, ongoing praise as described in God's Word has been, for the most part, overlooked.[2]

## Praise As a Lifestyle

*To be most life-changing, praise must be huge, overflowing, ongoing, a fixed (steady) habit — a full-time job, a total way of life.* This truth is emphasized in Psalm 57:7: "My heart is *fixed*, O God, my heart is *fixed*; I *will* sing, yea, I will give praise" (ASV). This verse tells us David had decided in his heart to praise God, no matter what. We are told, in fact, when David wrote this psalm he was running from King's Saul's angry chase. David praised God because it was a part of him, something he did day in and day out; praise was not something he did just when he felt like it. Praise had become a full-time job for him, just like it was for those special living creatures praising God day and night in heaven (Rev. 4:8).

# Praising God for Everything

Praising God for everything that comes into our lives is not always easy. This kind of praise does not just happen. Praise is easy when things are going well. It is natural to praise God for good things. It is perfectly normal to be happy and thankful for success, a good salary, good health, and popularity. Yet, David praised God while his life was in danger. He was doing what the apostle Paul says we should do: "give thanks *always for all things*" (Eph. 5:20). And this verse seems to include things that are not so nice, things that may be painful, embarrassing and even tragic or dangerous.

# There Is a Reason for Praise That Never Stops

*We are inspired and encouraged to praise God all the time, because of His unchanging character and goodness.* We know we can count on Him to do the right thing. He will always love us, care for us and do what is best for us. If Satan had been successful in trying to take God off His throne, almighty selfishness — instead of Almighty Love — would be on the throne of the universe. If Satan had won, our lives would be at the mercy of almighty hate and cruelty. Instead of a hell with boundaries, the whole universe would be hell.

Thank God, Satan lost. Today, there is a heart at the heart of the universe. "The hands that were pierced do move the wheels of human history and mold the circumstances of individual lives" (Maclaren). As David said in Psalm 31:15, "My future is in your hands" (NLT). *Because Almighty Love rules, all who are held in His arms are kept safe and the evil one cannot touch them* (1 John 5:18). *Nothing that is truly evil can possibly reach a true Christian because Almighty Love is behind the scenes making sure everything, both evil and good, works out for the best for God's beloved child. This includes all those things that seem most evil, even the mistakes of the Christian himself.*

## Praise As a Sacrifice

How can a person offer God a sacrifice of praise? Hebrews 13:15 gives us the key: "Through Jesus, therefore, let us *continually* offer to God a *sacrifice* of praise — the fruit of lips that confess his name" (NIV). What is meant by "a sacrifice of praise?" A sacrifice calls for death. In the Old Testament ceremony it was an animal that died, but in the "sacrifice of praise" it is the personal ego that must die. *A person must sacrifice or give up his own judgment, his own opinion, his own idea of what is right and good, and praise God always for all things including the good, the bad, and the indifferent.* The "fruit of lips" means the sacrifice of praise is not complete until it is expressed with words.

We have each been victim of circumstances that are sad, hurtful, tragic, or unfair — conditions in which we can see nothing good, only evil. It is humanly impossible to see how any good purpose can come out of such circumstances. During such times, in such circumstances, we must offer the sacrifice of praise. *The only time a person can offer the sacrifice of praise is when things seem to be going wrong, for it is only then we are asked to die to our own opinions, choices and common sense.*

# What Kind of Faith
# Offers Praise All the Time?

When a Christian offers the sacrifice of praise, he must take hold of the faith that God is both good and all-powerful; he must grasp the faith that knows how to "be still and know that [He is] God" (Psa. 46:10, NIV). This faith knows the universe has no loose ends. It knows Satan can never sneak up on the blind side of God, because He is the One Who sees everything. This faith is sure that God rules over everything and can outsmart Satan, not in some, but in *all* problems and dilemmas Satan's evil mind devises and tries to execute.

# Praise Drives Out the
# "Evil" From Any Situation

Since all the evil in any situation is always because of Satan's presence and activity — and since he is allergic to praise — strong, victorious praise drives him out, just as it drove him out of heaven. When Satan leaves, the evil leaves also. Even if the situation does not change, the evil is taken out — the poison is removed. The idea that "praise *always* changes circumstances" is a mistake. It may not always change circumstances, but it *will* change the person doing the praising. *Since the root of all our problems is the sinful ego, inside change may be more important than changed circumstances.*

Therefore, when we offer to God the sacrifice of praise we are acting in faith, believing that nothing but good can come to God's children, no matter how evil a circumstance may seem. The assurance that all things — including what seems to be evil — are working for our good, is surely enough reason to make praise a way of life.

# Praising for Cancer

Amy Carmichael, poet and missionary to India, said the eternal meaning of a thing or a circumstance is not in the thing itself but in our reaction to it. The stressful situation will go away eventually, but our reaction to it will affect our character morally and spiritually for a long time to come. Satan's goal is for trials to drive us away from God and cause us to sit in judgment of Him — questioning His motive, His goodness and His justice. Satan lies about God by suggesting He hasn't treated us fairly; he suggests that if He was all good and all powerful He would never let such sorrow or hurt come our way.

When we listen to and accept Satan's suggestions and begin to doubt God's faithfulness and goodness, we then begin to rebel against God in our heart and our character slowly weakens and decays. This is what Satan wants; when he sees this happening to us he knows he has won.

There is good news. When we let problems, hurts or sorrows push us *toward* God the effect is just the opposite. How can we do this? We must believe that our troubles come from the hand of a wise, loving, all-powerful God who always works everything out for our good. In spite of how things appear, we must praise God believing nothing truly evil can ever come to one of His children. *This reaction will make us stronger and will build up all the best, godlike qualities in our character.* When we respond to life's hard places in faith and praise, God wins — His purposes are accomplished — and Satan loses.

*When we respond to hard times with praise, those same negative experiences leave us stronger in faith, courage, and in our understanding of God.* Thus, a woman who finds her way back to God because of her personal battle with cancer can say, "I have been richly blessed by cancer." It also helps us understand a piece of advice by Alexander Maclaren: "Don't waste your sorrows." Likewise, Watchman Nee claims that a person never learns anything new about God except through hardship.

Yes, a God who can take all evil — even our own human mistakes — and, by His love and grace, turn them into weapons against Satan, make our character better and stronger, and bring glory to His own name, is a God we should thank and praise all the time. As Paul instructs in Ephesians 5:20, it makes sense to "give thanks for everything to God the Father in the name of our Lord Jesus Christ" (NLT). God's ability to turn our darkness into light is the basis for believing that nothing truly evil can come to His children.[3] God beautifully promises us in Psalm 91:9-10, "If you make the LORD your refuge, if you make the Most High your shelter, no evil will conquer you; no plague will come near your home" (NLT).

## Praise Is the Secret of Having Faith Without Doubt

Mrs. Metcalf (*Making His Praise Glorious*) believes thanksgiving and praise are the sure way to win in *every* situation. This is a very broad statement, but it is both logical and Biblical. Remember, Satan is allergic to praise; when he is ushered out of a situation because of praise, our prayers are answered. After all, prayer that works is prayer that overcomes Satan's attempts to come against God's purposes. We can be sure if prayer does not get answered, it is because strong faith is missing. If our faith is not strong and victorious, it is because *ongoing, powerful and directed praise* is missing. Praise is the highest form of prayer because it partners our requests together with faith.

*Praise is the spark plug of faith. It is the one thing we need to get our faith up and going, helping it rise above the heavy fog of our doubts. You could say praise is the soap that cleanses our faith and washes away any doubt from our heart. The secret of answered prayer is faith without doubt (Mark 11:23). And the secret of faith without doubt is praise — praise that goes on all the time, praise that is strong and full of hope, and praise that is a way of life. This kind of praise is the answer to a living, dynamic faith and prayer that gets results.*

# NOTES

1. In one of his books, Pastor David Wilkerson shares a real-life example of the power of praise. According to the story, in the early part of his work among the gangs in New York City, he came across a group of boys on a street corner. As he came close to them, he realized they were getting ready to attack him. He looked to the Lord for guidance and kept moving toward them. At the very minute the boys looked like they were going to strike out, David clapped his hands and shouted, "Praise the Lord!" Surprisingly, the entire gang broke apart and ran away. The only plausible explanation for their action is that these boys were motivated by evil spirits who panicked when they heard the shout of praise.

In my opinion, this next story stands out above all others; it is the story of a well-documented event, which took place near Holton, Ripley County, Indiana. At the end of a service — during which I had talked about the subject of praise — an elderly woman told me this story, which her husband's cousin (a resident of the community, who held personal knowledge of the details of the story) told her.

According to the story, an evangelist had come to the local church to do a series of evangelistic services. To be alone for prayer and meditation, the minister went into a nearby field. He did not know that a dangerous bull was in the area, until the bull actually started to attack him. By the time he saw the bull charging, it was too late to reach a safe place. He did not know what to do. He thought this was it for him. Just before the angry bull got to him, he shouted, "Praise the Lord." The bull stopped in its tracks, turned away and ran.

What is the explanation? I suggest Satan sent evil spirits to enter this animal and make him attack this man of God in order to stop the revival that was planned. Yet, the shouts of praise frustrated and confused the evil spirits in the bull in the same way the praises of Israel's choir confused the demons motivating Israel's enemies (1 Chron. 20).

# NOTES

2.  It is generally recognized that one of the fastest growing denominations among Protestant churches is the group of Pentecostal churches and congregations. Usually, Pentecostals give credit for this rapid growth to their unique doctrines (teachings), and especially to their emphasis on glossolalia, or the gift of speaking in tongues, which they believe is the initial evidence that a person has received the baptism with the Holy Spirit.

    Many outside and some inside this movement have their questions on this point. Whatever one's opinion may be, it cannot be denied that the Pentecostal groups have rediscovered, for this day and age, the importance and power of praise. To the regular order of public worship — including periods of congregational singing, public prayer, and a Gospel message — they have added another important activity: a period of united worship and vocal praise. Almost universally, at some point in the service — usually just before the sermon — time is given for the purpose of worshipping and praising the Lord. At a given signal, usually by the pastor, the whole group raises hands to heaven and, with faces lifted up, enters into adoration and praise. This is not just a personal thing or an attempt to work up strong emotions for the sake of a thrill. Instead, the intentional effort of united praise and worship of Him who alone is worthy often *does* result in a manifestation of the Holy Spirit's special presence, which is nothing short of heavenly. It echoes the praises of the heavenly choir around the throne.

    It is my opinion, that its thoroughly scriptural program of *massive praise* — rather than its doctrinal points — is responsible for the great growth of this movement. No matter how a person feels about the subject of tongues, nothing should prevent any group from adopting the scriptural practice of massive praise. The Church at large should sincerely repent of its failure to understand the overwhelming instruction in the Bible regarding praise and give thanks to God for this

# NOTES

group who are being used to rediscover the importance of praise.

3. NO SUCH THING AS BAD NEWS! Someone has said that there is no such thing as bad news for a Bible-believing Christian; we simply face new challenges to our faith. As we grow spiritually, God can trust us with bigger problems. From our first commitment to Christ to heaven itself, this life is an obstacle race we are traveling. As we pray for and get answers to prayer for victory over the smaller obstacles, which Satan is allowed to put in our way, God permits larger challenges to confront us. These challenges are "God's hurdles," if you please, "on life's track."

Whoever heard of an athlete, training for an obstacle race, pleading with his trainer to take away the obstacles? God has promised some very wonderful rewards for the overcomers. How can we ever be overcomers with nothing to overcome? Let us show all onlookers — to the glory of God — that we believe Romans 8:28 and Ephesians 1:11; when bad news is given to us let us immediately begin thanking God that He is big enough, powerful enough, and loving enough to take care of this new threat in a way that will bring still more glory to His Name *when we have overcome!* (From *Temple Times* — Emphasis mine).

# 9

# Organized Action

*"Evening and morning and at noon I will pray, and cry aloud, And He shall hear my voice."* (Psalm 55:17, NKJV).

I f the reading of this book does not help Christians see the urgent need for a well-organized program of prayer in both their personal and group or church lives, then this work has not been worth the effort. *Satan does not care how many people read about prayer, if only he can keep them from praying.* When a church is really convinced that *prayer is where the action is*, that church will rearrange its group activities in a way that puts its prayer program at the top of the list. Instead of calling people to prayer spontaneously, because of emergency situations or needs, the church will use its best organizers and leaders to put together an effective, dedicated prayer ministry. The church that truly cares about making a difference in the spiritual world will not be satisfied to operate a religious treadmill. No, that church will see to it that *prayer becomes the main business of the day.*

Furthermore, the church that makes prayer its priority will also encourage individual prayer. In fact, the effectiveness of the church's group prayer program will depend on the spiritual maturity and depth of the prayer life of its members. Without individuals exercising a deep devotional life, the group will never produce great and powerful prayer.

## First Things First

Finding time for prayer is not always easy; it is a matter of priorities. *All of us have the same amount of time in one twenty-four hour day.* How we use our time depends on what is most important to us. We all take time to eat, sleep, and take care of the routine necessities of our daily lives. Most of us have to work. Those at home have to carry out the duties and responsibilities of household chores and caring for children. Even with these pressing demands it is possible to carve out time for a life of daily devotion and prayer that is very rewarding.

## Organizing Our Time

Each week offers 168 hours. After working 40 hours on the job, 128 hours remain. If we allow 56 hours for sleep, we still have 72 hours left. Counting 21 hours per week for meals takes the balance down to 51 hours. All of these activities seem to be absolutely necessary. Subtracting from that balance another one hour per day for Bible reading and prayer, still leaves 44 hours a week for unexpected things that might occur. I know this paper schedule will not fit everyone's routine; it is just an effort to show that it is possible to make room for at least a limited time of devotion and prayer. *Those who are disabled or retired have the time and opportunity to make prayer for others the most important part of their lives.*

## A Prayer Library

Of course, each church or prayer group will need to decide

on the best schedule and format for its prayer program. Keep in mind that *prayer must make up the main business* of the church, both individually and collectively. Every church should assemble a prayer library, which includes the best prayer classics. Many good books on prayer have been written, but only a few are classics. Here is a list of some of them. Books by E.M. Bounds are among the best. *Quiet Talks on Prayer* by S.D. Gordon, *The Life and Diary of David Brainerd, Praying Hyde, The Kneeling Christian* — these are only a few of the most valuable prayer resources. These and *others* should be passed around so the entire group will become readers of these important works.

## Prayer Plan Hints

In any good, solid prayer program, the mid-week prayer meeting is only a starter. Many other times and types of prayer may be considered, including cottage prayer meetings where time is spent entirely in prayer. Ladies prayer cells, men's prayer groups, youth prayer circles, and high school prayer meetings are all examples of potentially effective corporate prayer gatherings. Some of these may take place in the morning, some at lunchtime, some before work, some after work, some mid-morning — all are possibilities. Churches should also consider regular all-night or half-night prayer meetings, perhaps weekly or monthly.

Keep in mind, it is better to begin with a small prayer program that can be kept and increased than to plunge into too heavy a program and struggle and give up. The prayer program may include one day of fasting and prayer weekly, or at least monthly. Almost any church can have a prayer chain once a week or once a month, in which a different person prays each hour of the day and/or night. Some congregations may be large enough to keep a chain of prayer going around the clock for a whole week. The 15th century Moravians (who began under Count Zinzendorf) set an example for us. Day and night, they carried on a chain of prayer, which kept going with no interruptions for 100 years. This was the beginning of the modern missionary movement.

An effective prayer program may also include a prayer list — gathered, updated and distributed by the pastor to each member of the prayer group. Each church will need to find God's leading for its own specific set of circumstances and unique situation. *Remember, only those things brought about by true faith and prayer will prove real and lasting.* Everything else is false and deceptive — mere shadow boxing and treadmill walking. **PRAYER IS WHERE THE ACTION IS; therefore, MOBILIZE FOR PRAYER.**

# PERSONAL JOURNAL

_____

_____

_____

_____

_____

_____

_____

_____

_____

_____

_____

_____

_____

_____

_____

_____

_____

_____

_____

_____

_____

_____

# PERSONAL JOURNAL

# PERSONAL JOURNAL

# PERSONAL JOURNAL

# PERSONAL JOURNAL

# PERSONAL JOURNAL